RETURN TO COMMUNITY

The Voluntary Ethic and Community Care

Chris Heginbotham is Fellow in Health Services Management at the King's Fund College, London. Previously National Director of MIND (National Association for Mental Health) for over six years, he has worked in both voluntary and statutory agencies. He represents the World Federation for Mental Health at the UN Commission on Human Rights and is a member of the National Advisory Committee on Employment of Disabled People. He writes extensively about health, social care and housing, and is to publish two further books in 1990 – on human rights, and on mental illness discrimination (with Professor Tom Campbell). He lives in London with his wife Barbara.

RETURN TO COMMUNITY

The Voluntary Ethic and Community Care

Chris Heginbotham

Bedford Square Press

Published by
BEDFORD SQUARE PRESS of the
National Council for Voluntary Organisations
26 Bedford Square, London WC1B 3HU

First published 1990
© Christopher Heginbotham, 1990

Typeset by AKM Associates (UK) Ltd, Southall, London
Printed and bound in Great Britain by LR Printing Services Ltd,
West Sussex
Cover printed by Heyford Press, Wellingborough

British Library Cataloguing in Publication Data
Heginbotham, Christopher
    Return to community: the voluntary ethic and community care.
    – (Society today)
    1. Great Britain. Community care. Role of voluntary
      organisations
    I. Title   II. Series
    362. 10425

ISBN 0-7199-1257-1

Contents

Acknowledgements

I am indebted to many people – without them this book would not have been possible. The original idea sprang from a discussion with Jonathan Croall of Bedford Square Press after a speech I gave to the Councils for Voluntary Service – National Association (CVS-NA) national conference. He has been supportive and encouraging ever since. I am grateful for discussions with Usha Prashar, Richard Gutch, Tessa Harding, Amanda Jordan and Simon Hebditch at the National Council for Voluntary Organisations (NCVO), as well as with Andrew Purkis, recently at NCVO and now with the Council for the Protection of Rural England, and Foster Murphy, director of the Volunteer Centre. Huw Richards has been a constant source of friendship and ideas; as has Ritchard Brazil, David Towell and other colleagues at the King's Fund College. Continued contact with friends in the housing association movement has also enabled ideas to form. Without these contacts, and many more I cannot possibly list, this book would be much the poorer. But I must give the usual disclaimer – at the end of the day, I stand by the ideas in the book and do not attribute them to others, although I recognise that few ideas are unique and have not been discussed many times before. Any errors or omissions are, of course, entirely my responsibility.

I must thank Amanda Harrison for her patient typing and the computer support staff at the King's Fund College. Finally, I am grateful to Barbara Gill for her forbearance when the writing took up far too many Sundays of our mutual time.

Preface

It is often said that there are no new ideas under the sun. This is true of any social policy discussion, especially after some years into a new era and after a decade of a 'radical' government. As I put the ideas for this book together – ideas which I do not claim are necessarily mine – I was conscious of all the discussions I have had and all the books I have read. So much has been written in this last decade – the shifts and changes of public policy, the agenda of the new right (for example, Nick Bosanquet's *After the New Right*, 1983), new ideas on the left (for example, the recent Counterblasts series), the development of communitarian thinking based on the ideas of John Rawls and Ronald Dworkin (both of whose original ideas stem from the 1950s and 1960s). But the thought that nothing is truly new was brought home to me forcibly when, in the course of researching this book, I re-read Francis Gladstone's *Voluntary Action in a Changing World* (1979). He wrote of welfare pluralism as requiring a steadily increasing role for the voluntary sector which would

> include elements of decentralisation (more local involvement in decision making), destandardisation (more support for innovative and experimental programmes) and deprofessionalisation (more emphasis on informal care and self help together with a shift to prevention and the horizontal integration of services). (pp. 100–1)

Gladstone suggested that the role of government would gradually become the 'upholding of equity in resource allocation', enforcing minimum standards and fostering a pluralist approach through both fiscal and regulatory mechanisms. Ideas such as these sink into the unconscious and germinate, and sometimes you forget just where they came from. Noting what has occurred during the 10 years since

Gladstone's book was written, and looking to where the voluntary sector is moving, demonstrate a trend which must, by now, be obvious to many, but is still not accepted by large numbers of people. As the pace of change increases and especially if it becomes more 'discontinuous' (see page 70), the voluntary sector requires a strategy for considering its place in the 1990s and beyond.

Gladstone was right in stating that welfare pluralism will include decentralisation, destandardisation and deprofessionalisation. But the voluntary sector has not really grasped the implications of these changes. A number of voluntary organisations have become more entrepreneurial within a framework for achieving social result. However, there are some who have despaired of a Conservative government which appears not to care for the disadvantaged and which they see as throwing the care of the most dependent back onto relatives. Others dither and become so engrossed in the 'process' of change that they cease to produce outcomes of any value. The voluntary sector, as a whole, has failed to capitalise on useful collaboration. A 1986/7 working party, set up by the National Association of Health Authorities (NAHA) and NCVO, pointed the way to developing partnership in care. Three years later, it is probable that few have read their report (NAHA/NCVO, 1987) yet it is more relevant now than it was when it was written.

The challenge of being entrepreneurial in the service of society is one that the voluntary sector is well able to take. It must, however, do so in the context of a set of principles and a vision of the role of the voluntary sector within health and social care. This book is about community care – local, accessible, supportive services for people with disabilities and disadvantages (people with learning disabilities, people with mental illnesses, elderly people and physically disabled people). It is my contention in this book that the voluntary ethic of community care is part of a communitarian idea characterised by support for individual effort and respect for human worth. It functions within an interdependent society which empowers disabled and disadvantaged people through local networks of support. The 'enabling' state, centrally and locally, is crucial to this vision, but requires local people to organise in not-for-profit activity as a way of maximising participation and control.

The days of monopoly providers of health and social care in the private or public sectors are numbered. To be effective, the voluntary sector must not be simply reactive to events but must have a vision of and a strategy for the future, grasp the opportunities which now exist and try to steer current trends into a new path. It is proposed here that the way forward is communitarian, respecting difference whilst seeking cohesion. The voluntary sector not only has a role to play in services to people with disabilities, but also in helping neighbourhoods to become more than the sum of their parts. The UK is now a multiracial and multicultural community; for the next few years a key role of the voluntary sector will be to act as a participative forum aiding the development of a new shared morality – perhaps the highest common factor of shared community values.

Whatever the 1990s might bring, the voluntary sector is in a crucial position both to influence and ride those trends, by offering people throughout the UK – black and white, men and women, disabled or able-bodied – the opportunity to share in society. Volunteering and citizenship are mutually intertwined; the right to volunteer is one which goes with the freedom to be yourself. Our structures must encourage that right, whilst demanding that the state takes its full responsibility for ensuring that care, support and help is provided to those who need it.

PART ONE

THE VOLUNTARY ETHIC AND SOCIAL WELFARE

CHAPTER 1

WHAT IS THE NATURE OF VOLUNTARY?

What is Voluntary?

The term 'voluntary' is loaded with meanings. A voluntary organisation may be one which uses many 'volunteers', or it may only have
volunteers as members of its management committee. 'Voluntary'
ought to mean simply some activity or undertaking, offered in an
open and generous spirit and given freely without any hint of
coercion. People daily volunteer to do things, but we must make a
distinction between those who feel that they ought to volunteer and
those who want to help others or to ameliorate some situation or
another.

'Never volunteer' was the motto in the armed forces. If you
volunteered, you might get stuck with some task which you had not
intended to take on; and yet you could just as easily be appointed to
undertake the task anyway. 'I want three volunteers, you, you and
you!' is a standard joke about service life. However, it might equally
characterise the way many managers run their organisations. If a job
description can be stretched to cover the task in hand, then managers
call for willing 'volunteers' to tackle the work. In such situations,
people 'volunteer' as part of their day-to-day strategy of survival in
the workplace, knowing that if they did not they would only be
pushed into doing something perhaps less interesting or more
onerous. Can we really call this 'volunteering' when an element of
coercion exists or the alternative is that you are required to undertake
another task?

'Voluntary' has many other connotations. Voluntary patients in
mental hospitals cannot be considered wholly un-coerced and
voluntary. The very nature of civil detention always hangs over any
agreement to be 'voluntary'. In France the term '*volontaire*' in mental

health care actually means that relatives have placed a patient in a
mental health facility; a truly voluntary admission is known as a
'*placement libre*'. It can hardly be said that the patient was 'voluntary'.
Even if a patient accepts treatment voluntarily, he or she is unlikely to
have voluntarily become ill. On all accounts, he or she is not
'voluntary', except in the sense of not being formally involuntary.

Another form of activity which people undertake voluntarily, but
which cannot be considered 'voluntary', is providing informal care
for disabled or dependent relatives. Millions of people in the UK
voluntarily undertake to provide personal care for a dependent friend
or relative and do so out of a sense of love, duty or respect, or simply
because the alternative does not bear thinking about. The choice of
either placing an elderly mother with dementia in a long-stay hospital
or keeping that person at home in surroundings which are familiar,
homely, domestic and supportive is no choice at all. It is only
'voluntary' care in the sense that it is a natural extension of a person's
love or duty to that relative. If a real choice existed – either good-
quality residential care or the provision of welfare benefits at a level
which would pay for a high-standard domiciliary care purchased by
the carer – then the carer would be able to exercise such choice in the
caring task. Not only do the lack of alternatives negate the voluntary
ethic in community care, but they create a framework which is
inherently sexist. Over 60 per cent of (so-called) informal carers are
women, most lacking support in cash or in kind.

Are Voluntary Organisations Voluntary?

Many voluntary organisations are voluntary in name only. The
crucial facts of being a voluntary organisation are that the organisation is non-statutory, is or was established voluntarily as a not-for-
profit agency, and is run by people who give their time freely. The
only place where voluntary organisations *must* have volunteers is on
the committee of management or board of directors. The key
difference between a 'true' voluntary organisation and the burgeoning not-for-profit sector is that overall direction of the former is
assured by people who have no pecuniary interest in its affairs, but
are concerned solely, or at least very largely, to maximise what could
be called 'social result' in its chosen area of activities.

Expansion of the not-for-profit sector will see the development of
organisations which, whilst ostensibly 'not-for-profit' (in that there
will be no shareholders and no dividend will be declared), will

nonetheless be run by a small group of people in a position to use the organisation to pay themselves salaries and benefits way beyond what might normally be recognised as appropriate for such activity. It is possible to postulate a situation in which not all members of the board of a voluntary organisation would have to be volunteers. It is my contention in this book, however, that for any organisation to retain voluntary status, the majority of those who have the final decision-making power in the organisation must be people who have a non-pecuniary interest in the organisation's activities.

The Voluntary Ethic

From the preceding paragraphs, it is possible to begin drawing out some strands which help to define the 'voluntary ethic'. That ethic is one concerned with social result, emphasises good outcomes for organisations rather than individual material gain, and is voluntary, in the sense that it is not required – does not have – to exist. This last point requires further explanation. It should not be taken as suggesting that a lot of voluntary activity is unnecessary. Many people are sustained only through the work of voluntary organisations and volunteers. Our community would be poorer – spiritually, culturally and materially – if voluntary organisations did not do the work they do. Nevertheless, it is a truism of the voluntary ethic that it does not *have* to be; it is not coerced or required either through social attitude or legislation. The fact that society does not meet (or for many years has not met) significant needs in the community, and that the voluntary sector has not only recognised those needs but stepped in to meet them, demonstrates the importance of the voluntary sector, but still does not indicate that a voluntary response is *essential*. The voluntary ethic is an impulse to do good – not to be a 'do-gooder' – within the constraints of community resources and the rather arbitrary decisions on priorities taken by individuals.

We should constantly remind ourselves that many of the responsibilities of statutory agencies – local authorities and health authorities, in particular – started as commitments made by individuals through voluntary sector activity. Of course, statutory agencies also recognise new needs and respond to new challenges. The history of social work in the UK, however, is one of concerned individuals and groups of like-minded local people identifying community needs, developing some form of appropriate (often low-cost) response, campaigning for the adoption of the issue by Parliament or local government, and then passing on the work responsibility to local statutory bodies. Thus the provision of residential care, education, housing for homeless people, and the dissemination of information and advice all began in the voluntary sector. Child care is one particular example; another is the provision of psychiatric social workers. Large housing trusts, such as Peabody, and the almshouse charities (some of which were established over 300 years ago) were providing housing for those in need long before local government became fully active in tackling housing standards and scarcity.

The voluntary ethic is perhaps more important now than at any time in the last 50 years. To some extent, history has gone full circle. During the 1940s and 1950s, the welfare state flowered after decades of careful preparation when its shoots were tendered with care by early pioneers, such as Beveridge. Whilst the 1980s has witnessed a sea-change in attitudes towards public and private ownership, the trends were already apparent. In many ways, the UK has been asked to make a fresh start; whether it will do so remains to be seen. That new start need not be on an agenda written by any particular political party, but will still be a process of renewal and restrengthening. That renewal can only come through a two-pronged policy of, on one side, greater public and private investment in manufacturing, service industry and infrastructure and, on the other, the rebuilding of community participation alongside the establishment of a new moral base for the emerging multicultural and multiracial society of the twenty-first century.

The first prong of this policy requires and demands the second. Investing in the future implies individual risk and substantial resources, both of which come at the possible expense of fragmenting an already divided and stretched society. Without an emphasis on community, those risk-taking individuals will discover that they have no support from a 'society' of fragments, of unrelated individuals. At the same time, resources will be channelled into renewal and investment, thus further depleting the available money for public investment and community provision. The voluntary sector is likely to become more and more important, both as a focus for community participation – tackling issues which the state will not be able to address – and as a means of finding resources within the community to undertake much of that work.

The danger in such a future society is that the balance of community care will be lost or distorted. In no sense should it be argued that such care can only be undertaken by the voluntary sector, or that some cheap-option policy is acceptable, or that community services should only be provided if the voluntary sector can persuade local people to dig into their pockets for charitable donations. On the contrary, government has the duty to provide financial support to local voluntary sector activity as a way of enabling the community to sustain itself through a revised voluntary ethic; and that ethic or ideal must understand the need for this two-part policy. At the same time, there is no doubt that community participation must be enhanced as a way of containing total costs in health and social care, wherever possible through health promotion and the prevention of illness. Inter-sectoral collaboration for health care is essential and the role of the voluntary sector is crucial to that development, too.

Community

To some extent, this begs the question of what we mean by 'community'. There are many definitions; Hillery (1955), for example, found 94. 'Community' can be a social, geographical, or religious concept. Jean Vannier, in writing about L'Arche communities, talks of 'community' being about openness, support, friendship, enjoyment, and so on. Tönnies (1963) produced his now-famous distinction between *Gemeinschaft* and *Gessellschaft*. *Gemeinschaft* refers to direct, close relationships between people in a social unit, such as a family or tribe. In contrast, *Gesellschaft* is an association of individuals whose relationships are indirect, sporadic and superficial. Tönnies perceived modern society as a shift from *Gemeinschaft* to *Gesellschaft*, with all that implied for fragmentation.

Such definitions may not be very helpful, for most people will know what they mean by 'community'. There are, however, different sorts of community. We sometimes talk of 'communities of interest' – people with similar concerns who come together, even though they may not live in close proximity. Their 'interests' might be a physical disability, hang-gliding, or nuclear disarmament. Conversely, we also think of a community in geographical terms. Sometimes such a community's boundaries can be relatively easily drawn, as in a small town, or with considerable difficulty, as in large cities. Many people consider 'community' on various levels. You may live and be identified with Sheffield, but your community may be in Brightside – one part of Sheffield with its own particular characteristics. At the same time, people identify with a geographical location which may also form the basis for a wider community of interest through ethnic origin. For example, many Jewish people live in Redbridge; their community is both Redbridge *and* the wider Jewish community within the country.

Indeed, the term 'ethnic community' is also frequently heard. Because they are a minority group, many black or Asian people identify themselves in that way for certain purposes. That is their 'community of interest'. But they may also identify with Brixton or Southall as a geographical community of importance to them. For the purposes of this book, 'community' must be a fluid concept, though rooted in the two aspects of geographical proximity and community of interest based on ethnic origin or religious affiliation. In the urban environment, in particular, these two definitions must be allowed to overlap or our notion of community will be limited, becoming two- rather than three-dimensional.

Finally, it should be noted that communities of interest built on some leisure pursuit, say, sailing, do not help us to define a community for the purposes of providing care and support to disadvantaged people.

Government Policies and Active Citizenship

One of the main planks of the Conservative government's philosophy during the 1980s has been to slim down central and local state apparatus. This is partly pure ideology, partly a response to a badly articulated desire to encourage individuals to stand on their own two feet. This government's approach to power is through money rather than participation, especially in its attitude to participation *within* the community. It stems from contradictory implications within the Conservatives' driving ideology – on the one hand, a wish to reward individual effort, yet on the other, a tendency to centralise control in order to achieve this aim. Ownership and control are the keys.

Government has taken powers over the local state in order to enforce greater equality amongst persons. This may not be very obvious on a macro-economic level, as many disparities in wealth and power still remain – and indeed the poor are poorer now than they were 10 years ago. At the same time, council house sales and the encouragement to home ownership, the community charge (or pol' tax), the 'enabling' role of local authorities and the Calvinist work ethic are part of a wider programme of equality of opportunity, though not necessarily of equitable outcomes. Margaret Thatcher might not put it that way, nor do many members of the Labour Party wish to acknowledge the social implications within much the government has done. But it does not need much imagination to realise that a Labour government could use the levers created by the Conservatives to its own advantage. A Bill of Rights, entitlements to care and sufficient local government resources could rapidly empower individuals and community within a new structure of interdependence.

In view of the government's commitment to the kind of policies described above, Douglas Hurd's advocacy of 'active citizenship' was unsurprising. If the country requires renewal and reinvestment, then an appeal to philanthropy is an essential second component. But such an appeal met with a predictably cynical response, as did the Prince of Wales's ideas on community volunteering (see pages 33–4). Indeed, many people who have been involved in the voluntary sector for years were understandably offended that their continuous efforts had either not been noticed or deliberately ignored. Active citizenship appeared to mean that, having made a fortune in the City, a person should then give a little bit back to a local school, youth club, or health centre. If government is to appeal to self help and volunteering in this way, there is a clear danger that volunteering becomes coerced. Rather than moving towards giving choice to carers and the community, the likely result is to move faster in the opposite direction by reducing choice, and, for example, effectively removing options from those 'voluntarily' acting as informal carers.

Active citizenship is really nothing new, yet it is a concomitant of the trends which the Conservative government of the 1980s has encouraged or exacerbated. For some, it is simply a question of salving their consciences; for others, a natural response to material benefit. However, whether or not we believe that there are inherent egalitarian aspects to Thatcherism, there is no doubt that the world is changing and changing fast. Active citizenship may be a face-saving device for a government which is perceived as harsh and uncaring, but this does not make it any less real. The old consensus is on its way out through the back door but, as yet, no new consensus has arrived at the front. The house is empty, waiting for a new occupier – a new social morality.

The Need for a New Social Morality

It is the contention of this book that one foundation of that new morality is the voluntary ethic. Such an ethic has certain fundamental components which are common to most people, and there are aspects which will vary from culture to culture within British society. The UK is a multiracial and multicultural community. A dominant middle-class, white culture rooted in some vague derivative of Judaeo-Christian philosophy is not only under attack but disappearing fast. Latent attitudes of the 1950s and 1960s have given way to the individualism of the late 1970s and 1980s. This trend is reinforced by the growing ascendancy of minority cultures. This manifests itself not only in the strongly held religious views of the Moslem community but in the richness offered by these cultures, not all of which have a religious foundation. The UK has traditionally assimilated minority cultures from a Judaeo-Christian perspective, but this assimilation cannot so readily be sustained in future – a more plural society must develop.

The importance of voluntary agencies within black and minority ethnic communities should be emphasised, and they must be treated as equal partners in a debate with white agencies. The creation of a shared dialogue, which respects difference whilst underscoring equal opportunity, is essential. A strongly emergent black voluntary sector and a powerfully developing consumer movement in health and social care demand a recognition that the voluntary ethic incorporates the notion that every person is entitled to 'equal concern and respect'. This does not mean that people are treated the same but, on the contrary, in a way which is relevant to their needs and abilities. People should be treated as individuals within their own culture, but as part of an interdependent community.

A major challenge of the 1990s is to discover and promote the highest common factors that characterise a shared moral position. Tackling such a project would be a tall order at the best of times; at a time of uncertainty, it is made even more difficult. It is essential, nonetheless, that the challenge is faced, and the voluntary sector has a major role to play in the debate. If one aspect of the voluntary ethic is to encourage and enhance community participation, then encouraging debate about a community morality is an important task for the voluntary sector.

CHAPTER 2

MODELS OF 'VOLUNTARY' ACTIVITY AND ORGANISATIONS

The voluntary sector and volunteering is hugely diverse and always evolving. This was noted by the Wolfenden Committee (1978) set up jointly by Rowntree and Carnegie:

> We have been conscious of one over-riding fact. What is generally known as 'the voluntary movement' is a living thing. New organisations are formed to meet newly discerned needs. Others die. Yet others change their emphasis or venture into fresh fields. Relations with statutory bodies constantly change with new legislation or changes in administration. There is nothing static about the scene. (p.13)

Even the Wolfenden Committee might have been surprised at just how changeable the scene has become, and will become over the next few years. This chapter seeks to set out in more detail a variety of voluntary activity, providing a classification of such activity, and describing the extent of changes which have occurred, and may occur. There are five broad areas of voluntary activity discussed below: 'pure' voluntary activity, voluntary activity as a duty, volunteering as part of the political process, interactive voluntary activity, and organisations providing advice and information.

'Pure' Voluntary Activity

There is probably no such thing as 'pure' voluntary activity. The provision of any voluntary service is a type of gift; but such gifts between strangers, at best imply a form of paternalism and, at worst, constitute a differential power relationship. Giving and receiving must be entered into freely; our concern for 'voluntary' activity should not only be for the giver but for the receiver, too. Being in receipt of charity is something that many people seek to avoid, yet the voluntary impulse can, under certain circumstances, exacerbate the notion of charity and, at the same time, create further dependence. That aspect of 'pure' voluntary activity is one we must be on our guard against.

Many voluntary organisations delivering services to the community are inherently paternalistic. Volunteering in some agencies, for example environmental organisations, may not so obviously demonstrate this problem, but there will always be an element of 'we know best' about some types of voluntary activity. By the very nature of being 'voluntary', an organisation exists because a group of people believe strongly, even passionately, in a subject or cause. However, one person's or group's beliefs may reduce another's freedom. For example, campaigning to reduce the use of fertilizers may be a reasonable cause for those concerned with environmental damage, but will constrict the freedom of farmers. On balance, the good done to the environment may well be greatly outweighed by the potential loss to the farmer, but that is a utilitarian argument rooted in a form of environmental paternalism.

Such paternalism will always be present in health and social care. In these cases, the provision of voluntary care or support may create dependency. Instead of empowering the user of services to make choices in care – perhaps by giving that service user direct control over resources – the provision of voluntary care effectively reduces choice. This occurs for a number of reasons. People subject to support from volunteers or voluntary organisations may feel that they have to be grateful for whatever help they can get and must not, or should not, complain. Complaining may seem churlish and yet the service user may become resentful of being the recipient of some service over which he or she has no control.

At the same time, the very existence of that voluntary service may reduce pressure on central or local government to provide sufficient funding for other services: the local and central state, as well as the service user, becomes dependent on voluntary care. A power relationship is involved. By the very nature of the intervention, the voluntary agency or volunteer is accruing some power over the way in which services are provided – in the worst cases disempowering the service user altogether. It is not surprising that service users have been demanding a much greater say in those organisations which exist to help them, and the organisations themselves are beginning to see their role far more as empowering service users rather than necessarily providing direct care.

These criticisms of voluntary activity must be taken seriously. But the other side of the coin is also extremely important. Voluntary work is an activity given freely, often generously, by people who have no particular need – either for status or material gain – for undertaking it. Certain kinds of voluntary activity are directed towards achieving policy change along the lines of an individual's or group's beliefs, but much voluntary activity in health, social care, education and the environment is built on a desire to improve the world and to help others. We should not deny the importance of such gifts. Indeed, we must applaud the extent to which individuals within society offer themselves freely to help others or to improve the way in which society behaves.

We must, however, recognise that, in one sense, 'pure' voluntary activity can never really exist. A person may volunteer, apparently freely, to undertake a particular task, but this does not make it an entirely selfless act. Often the person who volunteers obtains something from the act of volunteering – even if it is simply a feeling of doing good. We must, in no sense, castigate the person who enjoys the voluntary task – indeed, we can reasonably suggest that people should not volunteer to serve the community unless they enjoy the work which they are doing. Nor must volunteers be denied the opportunity to get something back from their task. This may be in the form of training in some skill, comradeship with other volunteers and the recipients of care or service, involvement in some worthwhile activity which the volunteer enjoys, and so forth.

Some safeguards must be provided in those situations where volunteers or voluntary organisations exploit the disempowering nature of the service, resulting in unhealthy relationships. For example, child care organisations are now more vigilant than ever before about accidentally employing as a volunteer someone who might abuse his or her position of responsibility. In general, the nature of 'pure' voluntary activity does not generate these difficulties, *but* the differential power relationship between the volunteer and the person to whom the service is provided can be corrupting. For this reason, empowering relationships which are more 'user-friendly' are being built in the voluntary sector. One of the most worrying aspects of the trend towards more explicit contractual relationships between central or local government and the voluntary sector is the extent to which these relationships may be undermined by the need to perform to a contract or specification. This point will be explored later in the book.

In summary, voluntary activity is rarely pure. We think of straightforward volunteering as being a natural *impulse* to help others or some cause. Rarely, if ever, will this volunteering be totally disinterested; and there is no reason why it should be. Some measure of non-monetary reward for the voluntary task (and even small sums by way of expenses or remuneration) is entirely acceptable.

Voluntary Activity as a Duty

We have already seen that many people 'volunteer' to look after a dependent or disabled relative. In 1985 there were some 6 million such people – roughly 1 adult in 8 – of whom approximately 3.5 million were caring for a severely disabled relative at home. The peak age for caring was 45 to 64 and in this age-group about 1 in 4 carers were women, and 1 in 6 were men (Central Statistical Office, 1989, tables 7.34 and 7.35, p. 134). Overall, women are just under 40 per cent more likely to be carers than men. In 1980 the Equal Opportunities Commission calculated that approximately 80 per cent of all carers were women – many of whom were unsupported in cash or in kind. Voluntary organisations concerned with carers have argued for many years that the so-called 'informal' carer should be provided with a comprehensive carer's benefit, in addition to a disability benefit paid to the person cared for. Appropriate pension arrangements have also been proposed for those carers who more or less willingly give up a job to look after a dependent relative.

In one sense, people *do* volunteer to undertake these caring tasks. However, it can hardly be considered truly voluntary when many carers consider that they have little or no choice. Not only do they feel a sense of love or duty to their relative (be it a son or daughter, spouse, mother or father, or other close relative), but they are also made to feel guilty by the state's agents – social work services, National Health Service medical and nursing staff, and housing agency workers – if they do not take on the caring role. Often the alternative is too bad for many to contemplate: the back wards of some of Britain's large mental hospitals are not the environment in which many would choose to place a close relative.

Informal caring is not evenly spread within the community. Pressure is brought to bear disproportionately on women, although, as we have seen, contrary to some beliefs, men are much more involved in caring than previously. Often statutory services make tacit assumptions that a male spouse or a son will not be in a position to, want to, or be able to look after a frail or dependent relative, whereas no such inhibitions normally attend their attitude towards wives or daughters. The sexism inherent in these decisions is usually quite blatant, reinforced by social attitudes which, in themselves, bring further pressure onto people already conditioned to accept a caring role. The last 20 years have seen attitudes shift, but there is still significant pressure on women to undertake these caring tasks. As women become more active in the workforce, additional problems may develop. Further demographic change will put pressure on both statutory and not-for-profit services to provide the care previously undertaken by female relatives.

For our present purposes, we must recognise that the epithet 'voluntary' is often misapplied to the nature of these tasks. A person may take on caring work voluntarily, but only because of a range of significant pressures which add up to a form of coercion. This should not be taken to imply that the work is unimportant, nor that people do not genuinely care for their relatives. Many would argue that it is right for them to undertake such caring and, on one level, that should not be challenged.

Analysing the extent to which the activity is voluntary does not demean the nature of the care provided nor the honourable impulses which underpin it. We must, however, be rigorous in noting that, to a large extent, such caring is not voluntary – and yet it forms a significant and growing proportion of community health and social care. Indeed, a large element of the current government's philosophy is to shift the burden of care from state institutions onto families and informal carers. Encouraging active citizenship and voluntary activity by families is, in part, an exercise to encourage families, some would say by using moral blackmail, to undertake caring tasks which they might not otherwise feel were their responsibility.

In order to develop the not-for-profit and voluntary sectors in the 1990s, it is important to clarify what is meant by 'voluntary'. A voluntary agency may have been established voluntarily to assist in community care, but its role is not necessarily to co-ordinate 'coerced' volunteers. Allowing the state, by a sleight of hand, to shift the burden of care onto volunteers must be resisted. So should any attempt to develop voluntary agencies solely for this purpose. Any movement away from genuine volunteering to enforcement is unacceptable, as my discussion of the 'community army' in chapter 3 will point out. Being clear that informal caring is not a 'voluntary' activity will help us to define a stance for the voluntary sector in relation to these trends.

Finally, we may note another form of voluntary activity as duty. Some voluntary organisations require staff to 'volunteer' to work in the evenings and at weekends for no additional remuneration, although they may be allowed time off in lieu. It is in the nature of such organisations that a certain amount of 'voluntary' time is required as a duty associated with the job, but it is not really voluntary. It is a form of 'required voluntary' time and, whilst the term 'coercion' may not be quite appropriate, neither is it reasonable to use the term 'voluntary'.

Volunteering in the Political Process

The attitude of political parties to volunteering varies across the political spectrum.

The Political Right

The political right – that is, the Monday Club, the 'No Turning Back' group, and those who support similar positions, such as the Adam Smith Institute and philosophers like Hayek and Nozick – takes the view that volunteering is a mixture of 'pure' voluntary activity and duty. The state should provide only what has been called a 'night watchman society', incorporating a very low safety net. Anybody requiring care or support, help or attention over and above the level of that safety net would have to get help from charitable or voluntary agencies. Many people would thus be forced into 'volunteering' or, more precisely, undertaking work for free. Hayek has stated that voluntary activity is the 'true expression of welfare'; and similar attitudes partly explain the drive over recent years towards the voluntarisation and privatisation of welfare.

However, contradictory trends have emerged during the 1980s. The later years of the decade have seen ideas developing in social care along the lines first proposed formally by Sir Roy Griffiths (1988) in his report, *Community Care: An Agenda for Action*. Whilst a trend to means-testing care can be discerned, the core ideal of the Griffiths Report was that statutory agencies should assess an individual's needs and construct a package of care relevant to those needs. The agency should then ensure that the required package is delivered, if necessary buying in care from a range of private and voluntary agencies. By and large, this is an attempt to cut the overall cost per service user whilst, at the same time, using resources most effectively. On the one hand, the Griffiths' ideal is absolutely right (ensuring services are relevant and responsive to an individual's unique needs) whilst, on the other hand, the tendency will be there to maximise the use of free resources (families, informal carers and voluntary agencies) as a way of minimising the cost per client.

The Political Left

The political left has traditionally been suspicious of the voluntary sector. Voluntary organisations are perceived as 'flower-hatted do-gooders' and, as if forming a mirror image of the political right's view, the left perceives voluntary organisations as expressions of a politically conservative community. This is a naïve viewpoint, however, and the Labour Party and left-wing councils have become more sophisticated in recent years. Some, like the London Borough of Camden, have for many years funded voluntary activity to a very large extent. For example, Camden Council's 'soft-left' policies in the 1970s encouraged the involvement of community groups within a framework of considerable statutory expenditure.

However, as cuts in local government expenditure have bitten during the 1980s, local councils like Camden have been faced with harsh decisions about financial priorities. The voluntary sector cannot be expected to carry the burden alone if statutory services and funds to voluntary agencies are cut back. The interdependence of the voluntary and statutory sectors is an important aspect of health and social care provision in boroughs such as Camden. If voluntary activity is cut, important sections of service provision are sliced out.

In other boroughs, the voluntary sector is less sympathetically viewed. For example, Barking and Dagenham give very little funding to the voluntary sector. It is expected to be voluntary *and* volunteer, tolerated but hardly noticed by Members and officers alike. To many on the left of the Labour Party, the voluntary sector is an obstacle undermining the importance of state provision for those with significant needs. Local authorities run on such principles may be unable to provide all the services that people require but, at the same time, be ideologically opposed to developing voluntary activity. Ironically, of course, political parties are some of the largest voluntary organisations in the country.

If the political left's view of the voluntary sector has been antagonistic in the past, the 1980s drive for pluralism and not-for-profit activity is complete anathema. The new pluralism is seen as the thin end of the wedge of privatisation, potentially undermining statutory provision – what might be termed 'state' production. Although many left-wing councils are coming to terms with the changes, especially those brought about by the Griffiths proposals and the development of care management, nonetheless many continue to look askance at voluntary activity. Indeed, the voluntary sector itself must make sure that it is not made the scapegoat for any failures of community care. Much of the present government's rhetoric is aimed at encouraging private and voluntary activity, but the voluntary sector must be cautious in those areas where its future could be threatened by changes of party or policy in central government. Some changes and trends cannot be reversed; others might be.

The Political Centre

The Social and Liberal Democrats' view of the voluntary sector is both confusing and inappropriate. In many ways, the voluntary sector is the embodiment of the centre-left liberal democratic consensus. Liberalism in British politics is substantially tinged with communitarian (see pages 41–2) or even socialist principles, and is not the out-and-out, right-wing liberalism associated with classical economics. What characterises the centre ground, however, is the breadth of political view from those who might espouse old-fashioned liberalism through to those who take a much more statist or interventionist role. The voluntary sector as the focus of community activity might be thought to be more firmly in the liberal-democratic camp than any other. Nevertheless, in its manifesto on community care in 1986, the Social Democratic Party (SDP) undermined that view by suggesting that the way to fund health service provision was through a much more extensive use of volunteers. Some of these would be unemployed people coerced to volunteer in health and social care in order to earn their welfare benefits.

A strange lack of understanding is evident in the British political centre of the communitarian possibilities inherent in the changes which the present Conservative government has brought about. In particular, the changes proposed by Sir Roy Griffiths (1988), government's response to the Griffiths Report, *Caring for People* (Departments of Health and Social Security, 1989), and the key proposals of the NHS Review White Paper, *Working for Patients* (Department of Health, 1989), might be seen as the vanguard of the communitarian spirit which squares with liberal democratic values. Instead, the Social and Liberal Democratic Party (SLD) has resisted the ideas in the government's proposals rather than demonstrating how those proposals could be hijacked and steered into a programme for aiding and enhancing the community. The SLD response to the NHS White Paper was entitled *Dead on Arrival* – hardly an auspicious start to a radical critique of government proposals from an organisation one would expect to take a more plural perspective!

Campaigning Organisations

'Political' voluntary activity is concerned to effect change, but this need not be through organised political parties. Many voluntary organisations were established primarily to campaign for a cause or to agitate locally or nationally for policy or legislative change. Although such 'campaigning' is frowned on by the Charity Commissioners (and may debar an organisation from registering as a charity under current rules), most voluntary organisations, whether charitable or not, undertake some campaigning activities. Any group which believes strongly in its cause will speak up in an attempt to get its message across. The arbitrary distinction between campaigning and other charitable activity is unhelpful. However, for our present purposes each is, or can be, part of 'voluntary' activity – indeed the voluntary ethic implies that communities should recognise need and fight for that need to be met, or be funded to meet it themselves. Whether this is given the term 'advocacy' or 'campaigning' is of little importance. What *is* important is the nature of the demand, and the local participation which it both generates and sustains.

Interactive Voluntary Activity

The fourth broad area of voluntary activity is that which we might call 'interactive'. We have seen that there is no such thing as a 'pure' voluntary task, though many people do volunteer in that spirit to assist others. Voluntary activity as a duty is not really voluntary at all; and volunteering as part of the political process is not perceived as voluntary sector activity and, in itself, colours the way that political parties view the voluntary sector. What can be called 'interactive' voluntary activity is a way of describing a range of voluntary activities where those who volunteer also receive some benefit through participating in the activities of the organisation. This does not negate their voluntary activity and, indeed, makes the act of receiving as well as giving explicit.

Interactive voluntary agencies include neighbourhood and self-help organisations, organised voluntary clubs and societies, and structured voluntary agencies. Each of these will be considered briefly below.

Neighbourhood and Self-Help Organisations

Neighbourhood and self-help organisations can be described as non-organised voluntary activity – although that might be a little unfair to those groups who *are* well administered. The reason for using the term 'non-organised' is that such groups are usually based on the provision of mutual aid one to another, and the support and help that individuals within groups can give. A recent estimate (Campion *et al.*, 1988) suggested that there are now 12,000 self-help and community groups in the UK. In Liverpool, the same survey found 32 health-related groups concerned with community care in one form or another (see table 1).

A typical example of self-help groups is the minor tranquilliser withdrawal groups established by many MIND local associations during the 1980s. Use and abuse of minor tranquillisers reached almost epidemic proportions in the 1970s, and only concerted encouragement for minor tranquilliser users to band together to support each other in coming off the drugs has enabled an effective response to be developed. Another example is when carers of elderly or dependent people join together for mutual support, both emotional and practical. The groups organise 'granny-sitting' services and help each other with many day-to-day needs. Other examples are women's groups, perhaps providing assertion training or self-defence, or neighbourhood watch schemes, which encourage people to keep an eye on each other's property in urban and suburban environments as part of an attempt to enhance community spirit.

Some neighbourhood or self-help groups use professional or paid facilitators, whilst others are supported by other voluntary agencies. However, may are small, local and established out of an immediately

Table 1   *Health-related groups in Liverpool*

Specific Disease or Condition	Catchment Area	No. of Members
Arthritis Care	city	160
Autistic Children Society	region	35
Coeliac Society	region	300
Colostomy Welfare Group	region	2000
Congenital Dislocation of the Hip Support Group	region	12
Epilepsy Association	city	60
Haemophilia Society	region	70
Herpes Group	region	60
Leukaemia Care Society	region	50
Lupus Group	region	80
Mastectomy Self Help Group	region	65
Motor Neurone Disease Association	region	60
Multiple Sclerosis Society	region	300
MS Painting Group	city	14
Sickle Cell Disease Self Help Group	region	8
Stroke Group (Liverpool)	city	140

General Problems		
Cancer Care Self Help Group	city	50
Cruse (for the bereaved)	region	150
Depressives Anonymous	region	30
Leeson Centre (mental health)	local	60
Maternity Information and Support Group	city	65
Miscarriage Association	region	8
National Childbirth Trust	city	40
Supportive Help Against Drugs Organization (SHADO)	local	80
Umbrella Project	city	—

Health Issues		
Crescent '73 (mental health)	local	60
Croxteth Women's Health Group	local	15
National Association for the Welfare of Children in Hospital	city	10
Neighbourhood Health Project	local	—
Speke Women's Health Action Group	local	20
Storrington Heyes Elderly Group	local	600
Women's Health Group (Vauxhall)	local	50

Source: Campion *et al.* (1988), p.45A.

perceived need. Some remain small with a membership which slowly changes over time, with people leaving as their needs become less acute, and others joining when they recognise that the group might provide relevant help. In some areas, such groups have grown and developed and many have become the basis for substantial neighbourhood activity. Parent-to-parent schemes grow into providing regular child care and advice and information; black women's groups become the focus of consciousness-raising and begin to tackle wider political issues within the community.

There is no single notion of self help, nor should such agencies be characterised simplistically as either an individualistic response to welfare or as the necessary development of alternatives to the state. In other words, self help is neither a politically right-wing philosophy – the 'stand-on-your-own-two-feet' brigade – nor simply a collective response. It may have elements of both, whilst tending to be more collectivist than individualist. Self help must not be hijacked by a cost-conscious state as a way of shifting the burden of taxation onto individual endeavour.

Self-help groups are established because individuals perceive a need in other local people with similar problems and band together to try and meet that need. Being a successful and active minor tranquilliser withdrawal group, with a dozen members supporting each other on a regular weekly basis, does not mean that the group is capable of taking on the development of a minor tranquilliser withdrawal service for the whole borough. Research has demonstrated that professional staff of mental health services are so desperate for community alternatives to institutions that they may unwittingly put excessive pressure on self-help organisations. Such organisations are set up to support a small group of people, not to become a formal part of mental health services. Professional referrals of patients to such groups, unless done sympathetically and carefully, can have two unpleasant side-effects: the group may be overloaded and overwhelmed by the influx of too many new members too quickly; and the expectations of a patient referred to such a group may not be met.

Some neighbourhood groups quite deliberately expand out of self help to wider provision. Sometimes, this is a natural evolution as one or two members take greater responsibility for the group and begin to impose their ideas. Such developments may work well and provide alternative care within the community. Sometimes, the development is part of the natural process of the birth, life and death of groups and precedes the group becoming less relevant to the community.

Whatever happens, some self-help groups are able to continue and some struggle with limited support from statutory agencies.

Whether such groups should be seen as 'voluntary', in the sense we have been discussing here, is a moot point. They are certainly 'voluntary' in that their members attend them voluntarily and that any administration is undertaken by volunteers. They are groups established for mutual support, but often expand beyond their original horizons and begin to develop services for a wider community. The development of a voluntary agency begins in this process of reaching out to the wider community. Many existing, sometimes very large, voluntary organisations started in just this way. For example, MENCAP, the Royal Society for Mentally Handicapped Children and Adults, began as a group of concerned parents of people with learning disabilities. In short, such groups *are* the embodiment of the voluntary ethic and demonstrate the importance of principle rather than organisation in what we mean by 'voluntary'.

Organised Clubs and Societies

The second of our interactive voluntary groups are organised clubs and societies. This would include, for example, golf clubs and fishing clubs which, in one sense, are just as 'voluntary' as neighbourhood self help. They have little directly to do with community care – the subject of this book – though they are often concerned with the provision of recreation and leisure services, sometimes providing education or dealing with environmental matters and, under certain circumstances, providing direct community services such as child care.

Many of these activities are components of a comprehensive community service. It has often been noted that developing effective community care means doing more than just providing housing and domiciliary support. Leisure, recreation and education are crucial components of a service which aims to rebuild shattered lives or to offer people the opportunity for greater fulfilment. Whether we should properly see golf clubs as part of the voluntary sector is debatable, but it is nonetheless true that those who sit on the boards or committees of such organisations do so voluntarily and out of non-pecuniary interest – even though in some such organisations members of the board are paid honorariums or part-time salaries.

Structured Voluntary Agencies

The third category is what might be termed 'structured' voluntary agencies. Within this group, we could include building societies (as they used to be before share floatations), Christmas clubs, neighbourhood self-build schemes, and so forth. Building societies originated in neighbourhood self help, the first of our three categories in this outline of interactive voluntary activity. As they developed, they became more structured, and indeed developed into huge businesses. In most building societies, the majority of the non-executive directors remained unpaid until recently. The only remuneration was through interest paid on savings via standard regulated rules applicable to all. We would not view building societies as voluntary agencies in the sense of the voluntary ethic as discussed here. However, we must recognise the historical importance of building societies in the development of 'voluntary' activity, and that they grew out of precisely the same voluntary ethic with which we are concerned. Building societies demonstrate the distance which an organisation can move from its origins, whilst retaining some features which demonstrate the original collective impulse.

A Christmas club run by the local grocer is really no different from a building society, except it is on a much smaller scale and probably much less permanent. Credit unions, however, are more akin to the early days of the building societies. These are organisations, often set up in areas of relative poverty, where local people band together to provide financial assistance to each other. To be viable, they have to set down tight rules usually requiring members to save for some period of time before a loan is allowed. Members must demonstrate both good faith and an ability to repay – two requirements which used to be a hallmark of the building societies in the 1950s and 1960s. However, once building societies and other philanthropic agencies ceased to support the needs of poor people, loan sharks moved in often causing even greater poverty. Thus, credit unions are in many ways a communitarian response to the way that building societies have shifted from their traditional area of operation leaving a need – perhaps it should be described as a market – uncovered.

Another example of structured voluntary agencies are the Settlements in London, many dating from the late nineteenth or early twentieth centuries. Settlements, such as the Mary Ward Centre or the Toynbee Settlement in Tower Hamlets, are undoubtedly voluntary organisations, established as multi-faceted local agencies which aim to sustain the quality of life for a local community, especially those in or on the verge of poverty. The Settlements often provide advice or information (sometimes offering accountancy and legal skills), form a base for the Workers' Educational Association classes, are a focus for self help and neighbourhood support services, and act as an infrastructure for the development of community activity. In many ways, Settlements cut across the three characteristic types within this scheme of interactive voluntary activity – combining self help, neighbourhood support, education, information and advice, support in personal budgeting and sometimes other direct help.

Empowering Service Users

Interactive voluntary agencies include those which encourage participation, though many agencies which might come under the term 'pure' voluntary now encourage their users to participate in the planning, development and management of their services. Many organisations for disabled people have come to realise, or have been forced by their users to realise, that they must involve disabled people at all levels within the organisation. Disabled people demand that the organisations which work *for* them should work *with* them and be *of* them – that those organisations should see the empowerment of their users as a crucial objective.

GLAD (the Greater London Association for Disabled People) exemplifies this change, with many disabled members demanding a fundamental change in the organisation's objectives and government. Some active physically disabled people have established centres for independent living where *they* become managers of the support staff, rather than be managed by the carers. Habinteg Housing Association, too, has pioneered integrated housing schemes for physically disabled and able-bodied people in a way which assists integration and 'enables' 'self-advocacy', thus providing an environment in which disabled people can be themselves.

If the nature of the voluntary relationship is one which potentially takes power away from service users, then a concerted effort must be made to turn this on its head and develop structures which empower users. The 1990s are likely to see a consolidation of this trend where voluntary organisations will have to recognise the need to empower the users of their services – whether they be for women, for black people, for disabled people, or whichever group is the recipient of their care, support or help.

Information, Advice and Advocacy

Some voluntary organisations exist solely to provide advice and information, for example, the citizens advice bureaux (CABx). However, many other agencies provide advice and support, such as the Settlements, the Royal National Institute for the Blind (RNIB), or Relate (the Marriage Guidance Council). One of the key functions of local voluntary organisations concerned with poverty or disadvantage is the provision of welfare benefits information and assistance offering the maximum help to which people are entitled.

Many voluntary organisations are also involved with what might be termed 'advocacy', for and on behalf of and with the users of services. As health and social care evolves during the 1990s, the role of advocacy in community care will become more important. The proposals made by Sir Roy Griffiths (1988) in his report, and the government's response (Departments of Health and Social Security, 1989) suggest the development of a care management system whereby some staff member(s), within the social services department or health authority, will be responsible for assessing a client and devising a package of care relevant to his or her needs. The 'case manager' is then responsible for ensuring that the package is put together either from within the social services or health authority, or by buying in parts of that service from private and voluntary agencies.

Of immediate concern is whether the money available will be sufficient to buy a service which is fully relevant to the person's needs, or whether this will be seen as a way of promoting cheap options, primarily by pushing the care of disabled and dependent people back onto informal carers. To minimise the risk of this happening, many commentators have suggested that independent advocacy will be required in order to ensure that the disabled person obtains both a proper and full assessment of his or her needs, and the package of care which fully meets those needs.

Advocacy is usually seen as speaking with or on behalf of individuals. But another form of 'advocacy' is the role many voluntary organisations play in needs' assessment and local planning. Few voluntary organisations exist for this function alone, with the exception of forums, such as the Camden Consortium, which have been established to bring together professionals and service users. However, if such assessment and planning is done well it can be beneficial. Coventry Health Authority, for example, designed a flexible joint planning system which was geared to involve voluntary sector representatives. Four different approaches were taken:

through consultation on a specific care group with one main advocacy agency (e.g. MIND); via a network of agencies where the initiative comes from local groups; in public meetings; and via informal links with groups such as those concerned with women's health. This form of collaboration requires goodwill on both sides, particularly from the statutory body, though problems inevitably occur if one agency tries to represent all voluntary organisations, or is required to do so by committee structures.

As we saw in chapter 1, this advocacy function may be in conflict with the service-providing function of some voluntary agencies. Many voluntary organisations developed initially as advocates, but were then seduced into providing services, either because the statutory sector did not provide them, or because they felt able to provide more relevant services, perhaps more sympathetically. As voluntary agencies are encouraged to take on more and more direct care, a split is inevitable between their advocacy and service functions. This need not be a problem as long as voluntary agencies recognise the potential difficulties, and do not allow their objectives to be distorted without careful thought.

CHAPTER 3

VOLUNTEERING AND CITIZENSHIP

Citizenship

Before discussing the concepts of volunteering and citizenship, I shall first define our terms. 'Citizen' strictly refers to an inhabitant or free person of a town or state; yet the term 'citizen' has become imbued with additional meanings. We talk of 'free' citizens or 'full' citizens; we talk of citizenship meaning something much broader than simply the inhabitant or even free person of a town or state. Citizenship can also be a formal term, as in a naturalised subject of a state; and, although not a citizen in the technical sense, an 'alien' may be able to act as a citizen in a much fuller way than, say, a person in a mental hospital who is technically a citizen of the country.

Citizenship is attached in most people's minds to the idea of equality, freedom of expression, autonomy of action, fullness of life, and so forth. To the socialist, citizenship is the expression of that freedom which can only come from true equality based on sharing, without exploitation and hierarchical structures. Such a concept of egalitarian concern and respect should not require anything other than fully organised social interventions. Therefore, how can this definition of citizenship be in any way squared with the concept of volunteering?

Volunteering

The UK is a country which has relied on the volunteer ethic for centuries. The very nature of many British institutional structures relies on a concept of the volunteer committee member. Volunteering in the UK is a widely dispersed and diffuse activity. Compared with most countries in the world, the voluntary sector in the UK is highly organised, often effective, covers a wide range of activities and is deeply ingrained in British society. Even the concept of volunteering is poorly accepted in many countries and the 'voluntary agency', with its advocacy and service-giving functions, is quite alien to some cultures.

The Giver/Recipient Relationship

Questions are often raised about the relationship between citizenship and volunteering. Are the concepts of citizenship and volunteering in any way contradictory or mutually exclusive? If citizenship is about freedom, then surely this incorporates the freedom to volunteer to help others? Can any society, even one which attempts to generate the greatest equality, do without the need for volunteer help? Do volunteering and voluntary agencies enable people to express humanitarian concerns in the best possible way, as defined below?

Many of us feel the need to give. Chapter 2 noted that the 'gift relationship' does contain difficulties, however. If giving or receiving is not freely undertaken it distorts the giver/recipient relationship, creating immediately two classes of citizen. Giving must be free, but receiving must be free also.

Any gift relationship not freely entered into creates a division of power which undermines any attempts to build a more egalitarian society. As long as individuals still have needs, often subjected to means-tested services, any voluntary help can only reinforce their dependence. Nevertheless, until a social structure can be generated which does away with poverty and disadvantage, we must continue to develop services for those in need. Even if we had a society where everyone was 'equal', there would still be those who wished to care for a disabled or disadvantaged relative or friend, or wanted to help others who were less fortunate than themselves. There would also still be that natural human comradeship which bands together to tackle issues of common concern. Human beings have created many dangers in this world, but not all disasters are man-made. The Mexican earthquake in 1985, for example, needed volunteers – the human impulse to relieve suffering as it presented itself starkly and immediately.

Thus volunteering, if viewed as a way of enhancing the community in which it takes place, need not be a problem to those working to empower disadvantaged people or to provide civic services and facilities as a right. Michael Walzer (1983) has shown in his book

Spheres of Justice that pluralism and notions of social justice can walk hand in hand. Society may be imperfect, but that is not an excuse for denying the rights and needs of some people during our progress to a better society. Many people need help, support, care and attention *now*; the sphere of 'helping others' must be kept separate from the sphere of 'changing society', even though the contradictions are apparent.

In this way, volunteering is not only a natural human impulse but it is also a necessary concomitant to the development of a greater sharing of the strengths and abilities within society. It can also lead to a revaluation of the social status of those helped. Of course, this is a paradox, too. As mentioned above, if giving and receiving do not take place freely, a power relationship is involved which may well act to support the status quo. Yet the very nature of giving and receiving changes the balance of resources in a way which may enable those with less to make demands upon society for more.

The Politics of Volunteering

The 'new right' view is that voluntarism is the 'true' expression of welfare. Hayek (1960) suggested that volunteering is the *only* legitimate form of welfare. The left, as exemplified by Tawney, would probably argue that the only 'true' welfare is egalitarian social organisation. Tawney described socialism as 'a community of responsible men and women working without fear in comradeship for common ends all of who can grow to their full stature, develop to their utmost limits the ranging capacity with which nature has endowed them' (quoted by Kinnock, 1986, p. 11). One of those 'ranging capacities' is that of helping others personally and directly. The state can and should enable collective and purposive action; the state can and should create structures for true freedom of expression, devoid of exploitation. Such a state will need local collective action to achieve common goals and to share common resources. That will mean voluntary action to help each other.

Social services are both statutory and voluntary. Statutory social services have a wide remit, which includes supporting the best contribution of voluntary effort as part of a general plan for services in a neighbourhood. However much money we pump into statutory services, we can never legislate for relationships, friendships, neigh-bourhood interactions and local concerns. Helping disabled people, labelled and stigmatised by present society, requires integration and desegregation. Integration means friends, neighbours, someone to talk to, someone whose time is freely given to spend gardening, shopping, going to the swimming baths, to the library, walking, and so on.

Child care is a good example. Child care is usually freely entered into by people who want to have children of their own. Informal care is an essential element of society but, if a person has no natural relative, is the only answer a paid worker? Or is a range of caring, from the purely informal to the fully paid, the right approach where an element of volunteering is present? Foster care is a particular case. Many foster parents are paid in varying ways to support their task, but the task itself is voluntary, freely entered into, and most people would agree that it is a significant improvement on institutional child care. The nuclear family is not the only way forward: the kibbutzim method or the extended family both have their attractions. Each solution, however, requires elements of sharing and collective responsibility which imply a measure of voluntary commitment if they are to work.

Volunteering should be acceptable both to statutory social services and to any political party. It is a natural expression of one human's concern for another, whether it is undertaken directly or indirectly for the benefit of another person. Volunteering enhances citizenship by providing outlets for the skills and abilities which people have and which they can, and do, wish to use for the benefit of society.

Volunteering enables some sharing of power in ways which are very difficult for the established holders of power in statutory services to participate in. Volunteers can act as the spanner in the works, pointing out to statutory agencies the effects of their actions; but they can also act as the subliminal glue which holds society together. By its very nature, 'voluntary' activity is a channel for power, but not necessarily a source of power in itself. The volunteer does not have statutory duties to fulfil, and many clients will feel able to discuss things with a volunteer that they would not feel able to discuss with a statutory officer. That outlet is an essential element in any pluralist (or even socialist) society. Mental and emotional health, for example, is partly determined by political and social constructs, yet emotional distress is common to all societies. Would anyone suggest disbanding the Samaritans? Can anyone seriously believe that the Samaritans would not still have a role in a world in which social services had become fully effective in dealing with the majority of their clients? The answer must surely be 'no,' for here is an example of the best

possible personal volunteering aimed directly to help those in distress
from time to time.

Many current notions about volunteers and voluntary agencies in
Britain, particularly in relation to social services, are simplistic to the
point of absurdity. The voluntary sector is often seen either as large
organised groups, such as local societies for mentally handicapped
people or Age Concern, or as only 'volunteers'. Important as
organised agencies are, much hidden volunteering takes place. The
local ward councillor running a surgery on Tuesday evening is just as
much a neighbourhood volunteer as the person who cooks Sunday
lunch at the local MIND centre. The fact that the ward councillor is
also chair of social services, and perhaps works for a statutory agency
somewhere else, does not reduce the element of volunteering in her
Tuesday evening task.

Moreover, we should not be critical of the way in which volunteering can help the individual volunteer. Without such outlets,
individuals can become frustrated emotionally. Many people have
discovered their own potential and true selves through volunteering,
and have also developed their wider abilities. How often have we seen
the political activist rise from a narrow and constraining background
to demonstrate great ability, locally and nationally? How often have
we seen people change direction in their careers through the ability to
volunteer in one setting or another? But, more important, how many
times have we seen the individual, helped through voluntary activity,
regain his or her citizenship, and re-establish himself or herself once
again in the mainstream of society?

Separating our concern for the volunteer from that for the recipient
is not always easy, as each has his or her own distinct needs.
Nevertheless, in the same way that hospitals are provided because
people are ill not because people want to be nurses and doctors, so
volunteering must exist largely because people need that support,
even though the nurse or doctor or the volunteer gains satisfaction
from the task. The question 'who is the client now?' is ever present.
Volunteering can be an expression of need, just as much as the client
ringing to request a home help. No one should deny that need, but it
should be placed in the context of improving citizenship for all – and
that means working towards egalitarian structures which support
and enhance common ends, common concerns and equal rights.

The Dangers of 'Active Citizenship'

Despite my advocacy of the need for voluntary activity, there is a real danger that too much reliance on volunteers will undermine individual rights, unless these are guaranteed by the state. Thus the whole thrust of this book implies that statutory rights should be developed, enhanced and protected. *Laissez-faire* provision of voluntary services, even if supported with some resources for organisation and management, is no substitute for properly funded rights for care, support, income and autonomy. As Nye Bevan put it in 1948, on the establishment of the National Health Service, 'Private charity can never be a substitute for social justice'. Paraphrasing this, Neil Kinnock (1986) suggests the need for 'parity not charity'. We need, he said, 'social change not social relief, the eradication of inequality not the relief of its grossest manifestations'. This is not an argument against pluralism and voluntary sector provision. Rather it demands that people be given rights or entitlements to care; and that sufficient resources are given to local groups to provide the care that is required.

One response, given substantial publicity this year, has been voiced from a number of quarters, particularly the Prince of Wales. Under a similar theme to 'active citizenship', he has proposed a new volunteering scheme, dubbed by some as a 'community army' of young people who would 'volunteer' to undertake community service. The aim seems laudable enough at first sight. As the argument goes, there are many young people who would happily give time to the community if only it was organised and structured in some way, and if industry was prepared to support their activity.

Prince Charles's notions are not far from those of the former Home Secretary, Douglas Hurd, who has promoted the concept of 'active citizens'. In the *Independent* he put it like this: 'The idea of active citizenship is a necessary complement to that of the enterprise culture. Public service may once have been the duty of an elite, but today it is the *responsibility* of all who have time or money to spare. Modern capitalism has democratised the ownership of property and we are now witnessing the democratisation of civil citizenship' (my italics). As more than one commentator has pointed out, why not democracy rather than democratisation? Why not real participation within the community rather than what appears too readily to be yet another way of doing *to* the community? Douglas Hurd also welcomed the creation of a Speaker's Commission on Citizenship, aiming to add a 'fourth dimension' to the notion of citizenship. In addition to political, civil and social entitlements and duties, there would be a 'voluntary' component.

In itself, that last requirement is wholly acceptable: it is the context in which it is put that is wrong. Anthony Barnett in the *New Statesman* argued in September 1989 that slipping from the 'voluntary' to the 'volunteer' in this way is to move from a civilian to a military concept. 'The first is not just freely given', he noted, 'it is freely continued, self guided, autonomous and independent. The second is a form of conscription that avoids overt coercion.' Whether the term 'conscription' is reasonable is a moot point. But to reinforce this idea, the draft report by the Speaker's Commission suggests that new ways should be found to give public recognition to voluntary contributions – 'a new high-status non-political awards system' – an idea promoted by some parts of the voluntary sector.

Neither Prince Charles's nor Douglas Hurd's ideas have found much favour on left *or* right. Even *The Times* was moved to oppose the prince's idea. On the face of it, it may seem that his proposal matches the thesis of this book. On closer examination, however, the notion of 'active citizen' promoted by Douglas Hurd, the Prince of Wales and others is a highly individualistic philosophy. It makes little assessment of community and appears to be uninterested in community enhancement. It is individuals that matter, especially those who have sufficient time, money, or leisure to take part. If they do not, they will be conscripted one way or another through employers who offer YTS training or other youth schemes. If they do well, they may get one of these new awards. All of this misses the basic point about community development. Centralising the state, cutting back on welfare and then sending in an 'army' of young people to make good the damage, will neither encourage long-term voluntary activity nor enhance the ability of communities to be interdependent. This drive for 'active citizenship' is not rooted in society. In some ways, it mirrors the 'parachuting' of some national or voluntary organisations using Department of Employment money during the last few years. Instead of schemes growing out of local community activities, national voluntary bodies set up local schemes in a 'from the top down' fashion from bases miles away. Some of these were successful and it would be churlish to deride the good they did for individuals. Nevertheless, the schemes were not *of* the community, simply *in* it.

Thus the overriding objection to a 'community army' is that it is not actually about community at all. A tier is missing. On the one hand, there is the state; on the other, the individual. Nothing exists in between – local government having been subjected to enforced contraction, the community is seen as something of an irrelevance, except as the place where volunteering occurs. Whilst we need a new social morality, we do not require the type of moral rearmament which active citizenship appears to favour.

The ever-present danger with volunteering is the use of volunteers to relieve the gross manifestation of inequality; to place a pretty counterpane over the bed with no sheets and blankets; to make just bearable the gross disadvantages that many people suffer. It is unlikely that this will ever be the objective of the voluntary volunteer, though it may well be a role forced on volunteers if they are not careful, and it is one of the dangers in the new 'contract culture' which is emerging.

Volunteering, particularly within social welfare, is an important, though not a necessary, let alone a sufficient, requirement for full citizenship. An ability to offer skills and abilities voluntarily, enhances the volunteer's quality of life and, on balance, the effect on the recipient will be beneficial. However, volunteering in health and social care is only one resource and *must* be part of, or at least fully accepted by, the community in which it takes place.

CHAPTER 4

SOCIAL WELFARE AND SOCIAL EQUALITY

Introduction

We have seen in the previous chapter that volunteering and citizenship are mutually interdependent. The ability to volunteer is a condition of citizenship – volunteering enhances citizenship, and citizenship 'enables' voluntary activity. It might be argued that to restrict the voluntary impulse would be to restrict citizenship. This would certainly be so, if we have any regard for the notion of society as a community of interdependent yet autonomous individuals who are capable of undertaking activities on their own behalf and providing help, support and assistance to the wider community.

Whilst these ideas are important and help to underpin the notion of the individual within an interdependent society, they also come into conflict with the idea of social welfare and social equality and raise questions such as the following. Does volunteering undermine social welfare? Should volunteers be the corner-stone of welfare services? If not, what alternative do we see for society? Does the nature of voluntary activity undermine the development of equality by encouraging a differential power relationship between the giver and receiver? If so, can we develop both a theory and a practice which combine effective voluntary activity within the community and state-regulated assistance to people in need?

First, the confusion between voluntary activity and charity needs to be teased out. There is nothing in the nature of voluntary activity and voluntary organisations which *must* be charitable, even though many voluntary organisations *are* charities. Charities, by their very nature, must be voluntary organisations but voluntary organisations need not be charities. As we develop our approach to the voluntary sector in the 1990s, we must be aware that charity and voluntary activity are separable. Charity is often not acceptable to many people, although the idea of voluntary activity may be.

Political Views of Welfare

Many on the left will quite properly argue that people are entitled to live in a society which provides according to people's needs, and accepts from people according to their abilities. The state should act both as the enabler and insurer of health and social care. People should not be dependent on 'welfare' in the old-fashioned sense of handouts, nor on charitable donation.

The political left's criticism of welfare is largely based on two ideas: that simple handouts or the dole are a necessary evil on the route to greater social equality; and that social equality is achieved through the redistribution of wealth. In the postwar period up to 1980 that redistribution was undertaken by highly progressive taxation allied to the nationalisation of key sectors of the economy. Many of these ideas are now changing, as the left recognises that changes brought about by the Conservative government in the 1980s cannot easily be reversed, and that social ownership rather than nationalisation is not only more saleable politically but also a better policy stance. Any Labour government coming to power in the early 1990s is unlikely to hike up taxation rates to those which applied in the 1960s and 1970s. It is worth remembering that the (so-called) postwar consensus – notably the Beveridge Report and the subsequent enactment of the welfare state – was based on the ideas of full employment, that people would want to be employed, that there would be a very small number refusing to take paid employment, and that the welfare state would provide a safety net for those out of work for short periods of time. Increasing unemployment in the 1970s, and particularly the government-induced rise in unemployment during the early 1980s, demonstrated the difficulties inherent in this policy.

Various methods have now been tried to assist the long-term unemployed, many of which have not worked well. As the economy has improved during the late 1980s, unemployment has reduced but real unemployment (that is, not simply measured by those drawing unemployment benefit) still hovers in late 1989 between 2.5 and 3 million people. Government response has been to develop Employment Training which some believe is an antecedent to workfare – an American approach requiring people to work in order to get welfare benefits. Both the Labour and Conservative parties favour some notion of workfare, though neither has been prepared to be explicit about their policies.

The political right's view of state welfare provision is that, to a large extent, it demeans the recipient and that people should 'stand on their own two feet'. Many of the fiscal changes brought about by the Conservative government during the 1980s have been intended to allow taxpayers to retain more of their earnings and to encourage people to spend their earned income as they think fit on health or social care. This policy has been attacked as being all very well for those who are relatively well off (and who have never really been a problem to the welfare state anyway), whilst amplifying the problem for those on low incomes and for many disabled and elderly people. Allowing people to keep more of their earnings and encouraging the privatisation of health and social care may increase consumer choice, but only if the consumer has the wherewithal to choose. Choosing requires an understanding of the range of available options and the resources to pay for the option chosen.

Underpinning the Conservative philosophy is the idea of forcing people out of dependency on the 'nanny' state – a laudable aim if it were not for the fact that the very organisation of the state creates poverty and dependency. There is, however, an inherently egalitarian strand within this Conservative thinking which is not often recognised, but which over time could be exploited by the centre and left to reduce dependency on the worst aspects of welfare. The argument turns on the extent to which welfare is targeted; that is, in order to use resources as efficiently as possible to reduce disadvantage, some form of means test is required. Universal benefits always have a better take-up rate than discretionary benefits, but at the expense of targeting and the circular claw-back of a large proportion of that benefit through the tax system. Child allowance is perhaps the most significant example of a benefit which many people who receive it quite clearly do not need. The arguments in favour of universal non-means-tested benefits centre on take-up. In the case of child benefit (which goes to the mother), it is also felt that it redresses, to some extent, the sexism within the tax system and the sad fact that many men do not fully support women and children for whom they have a responsibility.

The New Order

The Conservative Party's policies on welfare during the last decade have left voluntary organisations facing in at least two directions at once. Many have difficulty in accepting a new world in which competition and user-accountability sit uncomfortably close. Inherent British paradoxes have become more apparent. The enterprise culture has created an illusion of material wealth, but although some people are undoubtedly better off, many are teased with rising expectations whilst living in greater poverty. Individualism has bred a more aggressive society, yet out of it, as we have seen, has arisen calls for 'active citizenship', and young people have given more time and money than ever before, especially to third world issues.

Consumerism has been the dominant theme of the 1980s. Quantity has given way to quality. Those who have, have; those who have not go to the wall. The new material consumerism is a substitute for the ballot box: who cares about democracy, if you can go shopping?! Voluntary organisations – not so much volunteers, but the organisations themselves – have become caught up in this new consumerism. Many have not considered carefully the difference between material and welfare consumerism. The material consumer cares little about the process of creating the product. Money buys all.

Welfare consumerism is somewhat different. The user of services wants to participate in creating the product, whatever that is. If the user has a mental health problem, participation in the process of personal growth is essential. If the service user is concerned about the community, only active participation will help shape relevant futures. To do so means local involvement, not just new, aggressive organisations where the word 'voluntary' in the title is meaningless. In other words, we are concerned not just 'to do unto people' but to see individuals as part of a participating community. Perhaps we should reject the term 'consumerism' in welfare and replace it with 'citizenship'.

The postwar consensus has died. With it has gone the old centrally planned bureaucratic statism. However, the alternative is less firmly fixed than Margaret Thatcher might like. Many people may relish a new-found freedom, but are not prepared lightly to give up hard-won and visibly successful services, such as the NHS. Some ideas have gained currency, for example, splitting purchasers from providers of services and extending quality assurance. On the other hand, attacking local government is not generally accepted. Generating competition within welfare, leisure, education, health and environmental services has excited some and dismayed others. Voluntary organisations stand to gain a great deal from the Local Government Act 1988. Yet many are tentative, frightened and unable to grasp the opportunities which present themselves – opportunities which are moving events towards, rather than away from, voluntary sector activity and organisation.

One reason for this fear may be that the role of volunteers in this brave new world is highly uncertain. My earlier discussion of the 'community army' provides one example of that uncertainty. Another reason is that pluralism in health and social care might be just another word for cheapness. However, there is no strong reason why the state should provide goods and services directly. Titmuss (1976) defended state production on the grounds that these are not 'economic goods' but somehow of a different kind, either because of uncertainty, or risk, or the vulnerability of the consumer. But Adrian Webb (1985) has pointed out that the communitarian direction (see below) (or the demand for pluralism) has associated dangers:

> The argument which has been central to social policy is stronger when expressed directly: removing the price mechanism allows service providers to place their clients' interests to the fore, maximises trust in the service relationship (and, inter alia, reduces malpractice suits, etc.), enhances solidarity by attaching tangible social rights to citizenship and reinforces other regarding behaviour rather than individualistic materialism. (p.55)

The associated fear that Webb sees is that 'private production (whether for profit or not) entails . . . a residual and stigmatised state service for the poor and marginal groups'. These fears are not groundless, but the positive and exciting vision of Webb's previous paragraph requires a different attitude of, and to, the state and the community. It requires the old order to be dismantled and a new one to arise.

The old order was authoritarian, imposed, planned and institutional, often with paternalistic agencies providing a monopoly of services based on professional responsibility. The new order is individualistic, leading to an atomised society. It is contractual and inherently legalistic, essentially about free choice and consumerist, but also fragmented, competitive and independent. Many people rightly distrust this version of the future. Perhaps it is no bad thing that the statist, centrally planned tendencies are dying out, but many reject the drift to an overly competitive society which the last decade implies. Somewhere between the two lies a better way – the communitarian approach.

A Communitarian Approach

As we discussed above, for the political left, voluntary activity is simply another form of welfare. It is seen as pushing people further into dependency and propping up an insufficient state system which, if it could be funded properly, would not require voluntary involvement. For the political right, volunteering is the natural expression of welfare, something to be seen as good and acceptable which quite properly reduces the burden on the state. My contention here is that both these extremes are wrong, unhelpful and damage the nature of voluntary activity. Voluntary activity can, and should, be a fully integrated component of the interdependence of people in society and should not be viewed as, or encouraged to be, a reason for society abdicating collective responsibility for the provision of help and services in cash or in kind. The voluntary sector has a major, if not crucial, role to play in building a new communitarian approach. Such an approach aims to develop a partnership between the state and community, between elected officials and local activity. This partnership requires a new understanding of the relationship between the enabling local government (which will continue to provide some services directly) and those expressions of community concern which find focus in voluntary sector activity. A partnership of this nature is the only way to deal with the conflict inherent in the development of consumer choice whilst, at the same time, ensuring that effective care and support are provided to those who need them.

For the purposes of this discussion, I shall call this new approach 'communitarian'. However, it is important to be clear as to what is meant by the term. Political thinkers on the left and right have tried to hijack it in order to put a friendlier gloss on their own philosophy. Some on the right have suggested that out-and-out individualism is, in fact, communitarian; on the left, communitarian is a softer word than socialism. Liberals have suggested that communitarian can be equated with liberalism – whether classical free market liberalism or the more constrained social democratic liberalism of the centre parties in the UK.

All these attempts to colonise the term 'communitarian' can be rejected, whilst accepting that there is a little truth in each of these claims. The communitarian ideal attempts to balance individual worth with collective responsibility, to fuse liberal economic ideals with market socialism, and to recognise the interplay between the central and local state, on the one hand, and the community (often represented by voluntary organisations) on the other. The welfare state consensus has been undermined by muddled thinking on both left and right. What is needed now is a new vision of a communitarian state combining effective, non-demeaning welfare with the empowerment of those who use state and voluntary services. This must be achieved through both democratic channels and 'real' consumerism.

The communitarian ideal will accept negotiated contracts between community groups and statutory agencies as a way of empowering local people. Local, not-for-profit concerns will be established by those communities and will be taken over by such activities as meals on wheels, support for carers and environmental issues, such as waste disposal and refuse collection. Disabled people can be empowered to undertake the work that they believe is needed *with* disabled people. Such empowerment will be especially important in assisting black and ethnic minority groups. Those communities with black and ethnic minority populations can be assisted to establish care and support *for* the community, run *by* the community, *paid* for by local government. In short, the communitarian ideal is concerned with empowering service users as citizens and as full members of the community. It is invested, above all, with enriching the community and making local people more competent through a deliberate process of 'enabling'.

Such an ideal is neither imposed nor offers the illusion of free choice, but it provides assisted options, including appropriate advocacy of those who need it. Instead of a fragmented approach, this ideal will be pluralist but regulated. Consumers as citizens can participate as equals and be given as much independence as possible, with support to take individual responsibility. At the same time, it should be possible to develop a real collaboration between volunteers and community groups. The motivation will exist to become involved in running local groups if people can see local service-providing organisations truly working for the benefit of the community. Volunteers will then be part of and in the community, not imposed from outside.

The voluntary sector is nearest to this ideal, but needs to change. Voluntary organisations value consumers and are responsive to local need, are plural and local. All of this will remain. The 1990s will, however, also require voluntary organisations to negotiate contracts and to work participatively with the local community in generating not-for-profit activity relevant to that particular area. The free-ranging 'do as I please' attitude will have to change. Jealous protection of independence will not do, if effective interdependence is to be built. Voluntary organisations must ensure that advocacy is provided and collaborative pluralism developed. Quality assurance will be the hallmark of the 1990s. British industry is already on the road to 'total quality', where all facets of the firm's operation come under examination. Voluntary organisations must undergo a similar scrutiny. A best possible volunteering will be insufficient if the personal relationships between staff and users are not good. A good quality in the physical aspects of residential care will not be sufficient; the quality of life outcomes for service users must be paramount. Voluntary organisations will have to think carefully about their advocacy, service and community participation functions and structure themselves to maximise their performance for the benefit of users and the community.

The NHS Review (Department of Health, 1989) and government's response to Griffiths (Departments of Health and Social Security, 1989) will speed up these changes. Government is intent on devolving service responsibility through tendering and contracting to a range of private and voluntary agencies. Such an approach will require effective care management, as Griffiths suggested. It will also need to ensure the regulation and monitoring of local agencies. An effective audit of charities will be required. At present, the law is confused as to the *extent* of 'trading' undertaken by charities. Nor is it clear what trading *means*. Not all voluntary agencies are charities, but many are and obtain significant benefits from their status. Entrepreneurial charities will require a sympathetic audit – support to undertake the job properly with tight regulation and monitoring. A truly free market in social care is neither possible nor desirable. This ought to be recognised or a lot of time will be wasted by trying and failing to make it work. Negotiation on supply must be an open-information process or sub-optimum results will occur, providing a poorer than necessary service to disadvantaged people. Both local and national government and the voluntary sector should welcome debate on what might constitute a workable regulation in order to create a 'managed market' – a market which will enhance the communitarian approach.

Society has always functioned by mutual interdependence and support. People know this and know the extent to which they and others volunteer to assist each other. It is why, with all the emphasis on freedom and individualism, there is still great love for the NHS.

Why otherwise would people volunteer, as they did recently, to raise millions for Great Ormond Street Hospital – a part of the NHS? Attacks on local government rarely meet with the response which the current government would expect, even if some are inefficient and wasteful. But no one wants ineffiency or bureaucracy for its own sake. Most people understand the need for autonomy to be tempered with interdependence, and that some collective provision is essential for a proper functioning of a reasonable society.

The voluntary sector has been, and remains, of vital importance in the UK. It is often the only way in which minority groups can be recognised and empowered. The 1980s have seen the emergence of a powerful and independent black voluntary sector; and disabled people have demanded and won control in those agencies which have traditionally spoken for them. The 1990s will see a consolidation of these trends. Agencies will move more and more towards the involvement and participation of those they exist to serve. Voluntary agencies must ensure a focus on the individual *within* a wider and interdependent society.

Contradictory trends have emerged. On one side, there is a move towards greater individualism, material wealth and freedom. On the other, there is an increasing concern not to lose the necessary interdependence within society, nor to leave informal carers without support. The trend from central planning to outright individualism is unlikely to reach its destination. A new community approach may well develop which is based on these two opposing forces – a rejection of outright individualism and a rejection of bureaucratic, inefficient, large-scale statutory organisation. The future should be about choice, participation, pluralism and locally accessible services, wherever possible under the control of local people. To achieve this, simply tokenist representation on statutory committees will not be enough. Resources will have to be pushed down to the local community, as only such control will be truly empowering. If existing local democracy can be fused with empowered communities then there will be scope for massive change.

The voluntary sector is in the best position to ride these trends. It must adapt to meet the opportunities which are emerging, to head off the worst excesses of individualism and to steer the trends into a new communitarian approach. Only then can delegation become participation; consumerism become citizenship.

PART TWO

COMMUNITY CARE AND THE VOLUNTARY SECTOR RESPONSE

CHAPTER 5

WHAT IS COMMUNITY CARE?

Community Care

Community care has become one of those phrases which means all and nothing. To some, the idea of community is an all-embracing vision of providing help and support to disadvantaged or disabled people within the community; to others, that breadth of vision itself undermines the ideal. Community care can also be seen as social care – residential care and domiciliary support mixed with a little day care and a dash of leisure and work services thrown in. The Griffiths Report (1988) on community care was essentially about social care – *not* a fully fledged community care. Such misleading use of language has unhelpful consequences. Some local authorities (since government's response to Griffiths – Departments of Health and Social Security, 1989) seem to think that they will be responsible for *all* community (health and social) care; some health authorities now expect local authorities to 'buy' health services from them. Neither is right; confusion reigns.

Community care is, or at least should be, a comprehensive arrangement of community health and social care dovetailed together in such a way as to provide as seamless a service as possible. Good community care will bring together those aspects of local helping services which complement social care in a co-ordinated and collaborative way. Community care is thus much more than social care, or that part of long-term care traditionally provided by local authority social services departments. Nor is community care simply an alternative to institutional care. This misunderstanding of community care is at the root of many disagreements between the professional staff of hospitals and those working in the community who are determined to develop a more local and accessible service. Community care, if it is seen as an amalgam of health and social care *in* the community, necessarily requires in-patient services for those who become disordered or in need of health care. It thus recognises the requirement for assessment beds and, in some cases, long-term, highly supportive health care for very frail or dependent people. The idea that community care, by itself, means shutting down the institutions and having no in-patient services is a mistake.

The 'Normalisation' of Community Care

The development of community care will vary according to the client group served. By and large, people with learning difficulties do not require hospital or medical care, except for those interventions for which anyone would attend a hospital as an in-patient. There is no person by virtue of his or her mental handicap or learning disability alone who requires hospital care. Many elderly people do not require specialist services and are able to live independently. As a person becomes very elderly or frail, additional help may be needed; but the person may still be able to live in his or her own home, given appropriate domiciliary care. It is only those who become very frail or suffer from mental health problems in old age who may require long-term health care. Elderly people with psychiatric problems will need a 'health' service, but it need not be provided in some form of institutional care. Instead, the service should be as much as possible provided into their own homes; and if this is not possible, should be within local, small, domestic, homely settings.

Mental health care services do not require large institutional settings either. The trend to community care has been derided by some as denying the need for in-patient acute care for those who become very disordered. A high-quality community care service would recognise the need for in-patient acute facilities – either in association with other medical facilities, or in small (albeit economic) in-patient units where 24-hour nursing cover can be provided, with medical and psychological help.

Community care is predominantly concerned to revalue and reintegrate people with disabilities into society. It does not deny special needs or the fact that some people will require in-patient health care from time to time. Community care seeks, however, to provide services in settings which are valued within the community as a way of establishing, encouraging, or enhancing valued life-styles and relationships. The stigma of mental illness is reinforced by the use of institutional buildings which, in turn, reinforce separateness. Only by developing services which are local and accessible, and which do not segregate people with disabilities, can a regime of care be established which enhances a person's human worth and dignity rather than tightening the screw of discrimination.

The philosophy I have outlined here is that of 'normalisation'. Many people have misunderstood this term, partly through ignorance and partly because the word itself is misleading. It does not mean making people 'normal'; nothing could be further from the truth. Normalisation is an approach which is determined to treat individuals with disabilities as people with the same range of needs as anyone else, and to find a way of achieving affirmative action which redresses the devaluations associated with disabilities. Normalisation should be viewed in conjunction with a broader political perspective of the care, support and treatment needed by people requiring long-term care.

The Need to Change Society

Normalisation is one 'sphere of interest' aimed at revaluing people with disabilities within the current moral and political framework. At the same time, many people concerned with disabled and disadvantaged people will want to change that framework. Those who believe that social organisation is largely responsible for the handicaps which follow from an individual's disability will want to change the way in which society is structured and operates. Nevertheless, the 'sphere' of changing society should be kept separate from the 'sphere' of revaluing disabled people. In one sense, disabled people will be in the vanguard of change because it is they who are most adversely affected by the way the world works. Yet to use disabled people deliberately as that vanguard is unacceptable. If they choose to be in the front line that is another matter; many disabled people are, by choice, seeking to change the world in which they are forced to live.

The voluntary sector has a major role to play in developing alternative forms of care which can empower and revalue disabled people. At the same time, it can act as a vehicle for changing society, without necessarily putting disabled people in the firing line. Voluntary agencies can both represent the needs of the community through their participative function, and provide care and support to people who need it. In parallel, those agencies should act as advocates with, and on behalf of, disabled and disadvantaged people, involving them at all levels within the organisation's structure. Revaluing people with disabilities or disadvantages into a society that they and others would want to change is like trying to hit a moving target. Voluntary agencies are pivotal to these developments. They can create a consistent approach to service and advocacy for and with disabled people, whilst also working to change a society which devalues the very people who are part of the campaign for change.

Let us take one example. In helping a person with learning disabilities to obtain a job, it may be wise to encourage that person to dress for interview in a fairly traditional way, and to present himself or herself as neat, tidy and organised. Yet the helpers may themselves not wear such clothes, or may at least be keen to change norms which they may see as inappropriate. An articulate care worker with a good track record may have no trouble wearing jeans and a T-shirt at interview, but the person with learning disabilities might. An example like this contains its own (middle-class?) value judgements, but is offered in an attempt to illustrate the problem which many care workers and voluntary organisations must face. At one and the same time they are assisting people to obtain the best possible help and attention, whilst attempting to make society more sympathetic to the needs of those requiring long-term support.

The Advocacy Role

In essence, the example above describes one or two facets of the complex nature of advocacy. The advocacy role is a major remit of voluntary organisations. In the past, it has been performed through speaking on behalf of people with long-term needs, even when they were in a position to speak for themselves. Slowly during the 1970s and more quickly during the 1980s, organisations for disabled people have begun to transform themselves into organisations *of* disabled people. Agencies such as MIND (the National Association for Mental Health), GLAD (the Greater London Association for Disabled People), many local societies for people with learning disabilities, the Royal National Institute for the Blind (RNIB), and so on have all found that they must change to accept a newly emergent, articulate consumer group. Many voluntary agencies started as advocates for better care for their particular client group. Often this was through the activities of parents or relatives who were not personally disabled, but were affected by those close to them. The 1970s saw gradual change, as agencies became aware of the need to represent more directly the views of those they existed to help.

During the 1980s, the accent of government on consumerism has given a sharp boost to consumer activity within voluntary agencies. No longer is it acceptable for voluntary agencies to say what they think without consulting the people they aim to help and, in many cases, disabled people have made significant bids to be actively and fully involved in those organisations. At the same time, we have seen the development of new consumer-only groups, as well as more equal partnerships of consumers and professionals. In mental health, Survivors Speak Out – a group of mental health service users who have come to prominence in the last five years – is an example of the former. The Camden Consortium – a mixed group of service users, professionals and volunteers working collaboratively for change in mental health care delivery – is an example of the latter.

The phrase 'equal concern and respect' helps us to think about the needs of disabled and disadvantaged people. Treating people with equal concern and respect does not mean treating them equally. It *does* mean that their specific and unique needs are considered and that help, care and support is provided appropriate to those needs. At the same time, every person should be treated as of equal human worth entitled to dignity and respect. Voluntary organisations, as participative organisations within the community, play a vital role in assisting the community to understand the needs of disabled people whilst, at the same time, helping and encouraging disabled people to be fully part of the community.

A Communitarian Approach to Community Care

The communitarian notion we have been discussing, which enables those who use services to participate actively in shaping those services, is an essential prerequisite for the full development of citizenship. The communitarian ideal is neither individualistic nor collective, but rather supportive of individual difference within an interdependent society. Voluntary organisations incorporate loose networks of people, scattered throughout communities, who act as a sort of social glue. Effective use of that glue can ensure that disabled people are given their rightful place within society whilst, at the same time, their unique contributions are recognised.

Community care is, therefore, something much more than an alternative to institutions and much more than simply social care. Community care is concerned to revalue people and, at the same time, to empower them to assist society to change in a way which will lessen any future tendency to devalue. However, community care is not necessarily about care *by* the community. Community care requires care *within* the community, undertaken by a range of agencies – statutory, voluntary and private – as a way of assisting and supporting people with disabilities and disadvantages. Unhappily, the ideal of community care has been tarnished. Because of under-funding, many people perceive community care as simply dumping disabled people out of institutions onto informal carers, mainly women. This does not, however, negate the concept of community care, or the exciting possibilities of developing a partnership between the community, voluntary organisations and the enabling state to create a more flexible and enhanced neighbourhood.

Although this vision is communitarian, it is not political with a capital 'P'. All political parties in the UK have theoretically supported the development of local, comprehensive care. None have provided the resources necessary. All parties believe in community care yet, for various reasons, their other policies have undermined a realistic future. As one commentator put it: community care does not so much have all-party support as no-party opposition. The Labour Party appears to believe in community care because it claims to care for disabled and disadvantaged people; the Social and Liberal Democratic Party (SLD) believes in community care because of its approach to community participation; and the Conservative Party because it is rooted in self help. Caring is not enough, however. Participation can mean little to those unable to participate (for whatever reason, but usually because of low incomes), and self help impales disadvantaged people on the horns of a dilemma. Many people wish to care for a disabled or disadvantaged friend or relative, many consumers wish to have control over the resources available for their caring, and many wish to come together to support each other in dealing with distress. Nevertheless, dumping care for others onto the very people who themselves need care is a cynical manipulation of the ethic of self help.

The Labour Party appears unable to commit itself properly to community care, partly because of a reluctance on the part of the major trade unions to see the dismantling of their power-base institutions. The Confederation of Health Service Employees (COHSE) changed its policy in 1988 to become supportive of community care, recognising that, as services shifted into the community, they would wish to recruit members in those community services. Their change of heart is welcome and it is to be hoped that other unions will follow suit. The Social Democratic Party (SDP) and

SLD believe in the voluntary ethic and local action, but often to the detriment of real services. Perhaps Paddy Ashdown's emphasis on citizenship will begin to shift that stance. We have already seen how the SDP manifesto in 1986 suggested that volunteers should be used to plug the gaps in the health service: where an individual was drawing benefit, it would be stopped if he or she did not volunteer. In some places, notably Tower Hamlets, the Liberal Democrats seem to have drifted rapidly to the right, becoming as authoritarian as the old-fashioned Labour Party they replaced. The Conservatives are unable to grasp that community care costs more (because it ought to be better), that it is not a cheap option and will not save money.

It is worth trying to obtain some synthesis of the position described here and that outlined in chapter 4. The essential argument is that community care ought to be non-authoritarian. Traditional right- and left-wing perspectives are based on forms of all-encompassing statism. On the political right, is the top-down imposition of individualistic philosophy which knows what is good for you – to be an individual standing on your own two feet in a far-from-interdependent society. The old Labour attitudes (whether of the old right or the so-called 'hard' left) are just as authoritarian. The 'we know better than you' syndrome dies hard; central planning tendencies continue. The voluntary sector has had an important part to play in challenging those authoritarian notions, and such a role continues to be relevant.

It is true, of course, that many people who work for, or are involved in, voluntary organisations are politically active in one party or another. It is also true, however, that the voluntary sector encourages the networking of local people. The voluntary sector cuts across existing political divides, is localised and draws on the needs of those requiring help, support, or care. Consequently, the communitarian ethic, to which the voluntary sector is well suited, is far less authoritarian. It does not try to tell people who they should be or what they are, to put people in pigeon holes by labelling them as 'schizophrenic' or 'mentally handicapped'. It is an approach which attempts to revalue people through involving them in society and helping them, in Katherine Mansfield's phrase, 'to be all that [they] are capable of becoming'.

Community care, voluntary organisations and the communitarian ideal all cover part of the same approach, that is, they see individuals as important within a local interdependent society, recognise the importance of cultural difference, and give a respect and dignity to all, regardless of race, culture, creed, caste, gender, disability, or sexual orientation. It is, of course, an ideal and it is easy to deride as unattainable. Yet, for many people who work or are involved in voluntary organisations, this philosophy (even if it is not always articulated) is at the root of their concern.

We shall see in the next two chapters how that philosophy can be made a reality and how the voluntary ethic, by sustaining and enhancing community care, can become the dominant theme of the 1990s.

CHAPTER 6

COMMUNITY CARE IN PRACTICE

Historical Background

Community care is, at best, patchy and fragmented; at worst, non-existent. Forty years of pressure for alternatives to large-scale institutional care have left a muddle of uncoordinated services. In some places, a basic community care has been achieved with the attendant closure of hospitals for people with mental illnesses and learning disabilities. In other places, hospitals have been run down, with little to replace them as community alternatives.

As we have seen, community care is much more than simply an alternative to institutions. Community care is a humanising impulse to sustain and, where necessary, rebuild decent lives for people with disabilities and disadvantages. In the immediate postwar period, however, when ideas for community care were beginning to emerge, the idea of the full-employment welfare society was dominant. The Second World War was a great 'disruptor', acting as a catalyst for the enactment of new ideas and legislation and the establishment of the welfare state, itself an idea with antecedents going back to the early years of the twentieth century. Received wisdom suggests that the closure of mental hospitals (and, to some degree, those for people with learning disabilities) depended largely on the discovery of anti-psychotic medication. The development of largactyl and the phenothiazines in the mid-1950s had a major effect on the ability of mental health services to sustain people with serious mental disorders in the community. However, the immediate reason for declining numbers in the large hospitals, from a peak of approximately 150,000 in the 1950s to only 75,000 in the late 1970s, was due as much to full employment in the 1950s and early 1960s, as to humanitarian ideas of helping people to live more normal lives. Many of those resident in the mental illness and mental handicap hospitals in the 1950s ought never to have been there. At that time, there were still, for example, many women who had been placed in hospitals solely due to becoming pregnant out of marriage. Even in the late 1970s and early 1980s, elderly women were still being found who had been placed in mental hospitals for such reasons back in the 1930s and 1940s.

There were contradictory trends as well. We now think of mental handicap hospitals as being firmly within the health service, even though many disagree that this is a sensible place for them. Many people have forgotten that the mental handicap institutions only became 'hospitals' when the National Health Service was established in 1948. Prior to that, mental handicap 'hospitals' were essentially workhouses run by local authorities. Many of the older staff of mental handicap institutions still remember the day when the existing local authority sign was painted out and the word 'hospital' inserted.

Services for elderly people have changed, too. When the National Assistance Act 1945 encouraged local authorities to provide what are known as 'Part III' homes, the distinction between residential and nursing home care in health and local authorities became blurred. Many local authorities have for years – until the 1980s – run residential care for very frail and demented elderly people. The health service, too, provides a range of services for the very frail and very elderly in hospitals and NHS nursing homes.

Proposed Changes

Changes proposed in the NHS White Paper (Department of Health, 1989) and, more particularly, government's response (Departments of Health and Social Security, 1989) to Sir Roy Griffiths' 1988 report on community care are likely to affect the boundary between health and social care. Already a number of health authorities are looking carefully at the provision which they make for elderly and long-term mentally ill people and asking themselves whether it is appropriate: are these 'health' services and, if not, should they be free at the point of delivery?

A health service decision *not* to provide has potentially very serious ramifications for many elderly and disabled people, and especially for their relatives. It is still possible (late 1989) for elderly and disabled people to obtain welfare (entitlement) benefits (either board and lodgings payments, residential care allowances, or nursing home allowances) at a level which pays for care in the private and voluntary sectors. Charges are escalating quickly, however, and a gap between cost and state payment is beginning to appear, especially for the better homes. If the health service discharges a patient to such a private or voluntary home, but state benefits cannot meet the full cost, then some top-up is required. At present, health authorities are not empowered to pay a top-up for an individual patient, though they can give a grant to a private or voluntary organisation to provide care for a range of service users. Some patients and their relatives may suddenly find themselves having to pay quite substantial sums of money, possibly causing financial hardship and creating poverty amongst those for whom the service is intended.

In parallel with these changes, the proposals by Griffiths and endorsed by government are to encourage local authorities to act as 'enabling' bodies. Social care will be the responsibility of local authorities who will be charged with assessing the needs of each client, devising a package of care relevant to those needs, and then ensuring that the package is put together from services bought in from private and voluntary organisations (and as a backstop from services run by statutory authorities). Existing clients of local authority residential care will have to be fully funded by local authorities, whilst people currently placed in private and voluntary homes will continue to receive those benefits for which they are eligible after an operative date of 1 April 1991. For new clients after that date, current welfare benefits (board and lodgings, residential care allowances and nursing care allowances) will be spilt into their constituent elements of income support, housing benefit equivalent (both of which are means-tested), and a care element. The latter will be given to the local authority to use in topping-up payments to residential care providers and other providers of community services.

These proposed changes have very substantial implications for local authorities, as well as for the private and voluntary care providers. For local authorities, they imply significant shifts in operation. Changes will include moving from a generic pattern of field social work and client support to specialist forms of service; from field social work operations to a care management service; from directly provided services to services bought in from a range of providers; and to internal markets in social services departments (that is, competition is likely to develop between directly managed units).

Facing the Future

All these trends have implications for the voluntary sector. Changes
to welfare benefits funding will put pressures on voluntary organisations to keep charges as low as possible and, at the same time, to
use charitable income to top-up costs for individuals. Trusts and
foundations already under pressure since the advent of the Social
Fund, are beginning to see a rapid increase in applications for help.
They are likely to be inundated in future with requests for *regular* help
with the cost of meeting bills for residential and day care. Already one
Trust has said it cannot give grants to anyone under 90! At the same
time, voluntary agencies will be encouraged to widen their activities
as care providers, tendering to local authorities to run new services or
to take over existing provision, and contracting with local and health
authorities to provide a range of care. These changes are not
complementary and will place divergent pressure on individual
voluntary agencies. Many have traditionally provided some low-key
services in the community and have acted as advocacy agencies with,
and on behalf of, service users for better care by local and health
authorities. Quite rapidly, over a period of two or three years, their
objectives and methods of operation will be squeezed. Whether or not
they wish to provide significant amounts of care, the pressure will be
on to do so *and* to use charitable and voluntary funds to make the
financial arithmetic add up. In parallel, their advocacy functions will
be undermined as they take on extensive service provision; and the
standards of their care will be constrained heavily by the contracts
which they enter into.

The Way Ahead

In the above paragraph, I have deliberately shown the 'down-side' of
the proposals in the Griffiths report. A more positive approach might
be considered, however. Many voluntary organisations are only too
keen to develop better services and the advent of the enabling local
authority, contracting with a variety of agencies, offers opportunities
to develop the type of care which many organisations have always
wanted. As long as voluntary agencies are clear about their objectives
and are only prepared to negotiate deals within those objectives, the
'contract' culture offers the opportunity for voluntary agencies and
their users to become more effective.

Voluntary agencies must be prepared to involve service users and to assist users in developing schemes and ideas which can be funded by local and health authorities. Assisting users to develop self-help organisations and new voluntary agencies, which then contract to provide elements of care, is a way of achieving real empowerment. Instead of scratching around for crumbs of funding, user-run services will be in a position to contract formally, obtain sufficient funding to run effective services and, in so doing, run services which users themselves know they want. Such services can be organised by users on their own behalf and run in such a way that the services maximise user empowerment and valued life-styles.

The same approach can be used to empower black and ethnic minority groups and to enhance the ability of communities to provide care, support and services to local people. Not-for-profit activity could be established much more widely, fitting in with local authority provision but offering communities the opportunity to have a real say, rather than token involvement, in the way care is run.

Community care at present is fragmented, although many individual components exist in different places. The NHS provides a range of community health services, usually via community units of district health authorities. In addition, there are outreach services from the acute units (for example, community pediatrics, community midwives), and grant aid to a range of voluntary and private agencies. Local authorities are predominantly in the business of community care, though some of their traditional residential provision leaves a lot to be desired. Voluntary agencies have traditionally provided discrete components of community care – group homes for people with learning disabilities run by MENCAP; small homes and sheltered accommodation for isolated or single elderly people (for example, provision by Abbeyfield or Anchor Housing Associations); drop-in centres providing day support for people with mental illnesses (for example, those run by MIND local groups); and work schemes for people with a variety of disabilities (such as those provided by the Shaw Trust and Stort Enterprises).

Rarely are services dovetailed together but, as the Audit Commission (1986) pointed out in their report *Making a Reality of Community Care*, the UK spends over £6 billion on community care for the 'priority groups'. The voluntary sector is under-resourced, but is crucial to developing competent communities which can provide significant support services and thus a major component of community care. The proposals by Sir Roy Griffiths (1988) and the government's response in mid-1989 offer a way to co-ordinate that service and to put money earmarked for specific provision into the voluntary sector. In doing so, the loose and often woolly relationship between voluntary agencies and local authorities may change.

Past experience of grant aid to voluntary organisations has been variable. Some grant aid has been entirely open-ended, with few strings being attached to a voluntary agency carrying out broadly and often badly defined activities directed at a particular group. Other grants have been more or less constrained by agreements reached (though not of a firmly contractual nature) and, in some cases, explicit strings have been attached. Although the development of contractual arrangements has its dangers, these can be minimised by an organisation setting careful objectives and insisting on a balanced portfolio of contracts, grant aid and entirely voluntary activity. Of much greater concern, is the likelihood that over time that money available for community care will be reduced, either putting a further squeeze on agencies that have been contracted to provide care, or forcing dependent and disabled people back onto relatives as a cheap option of care.

Many of those involved in self-help initiatives are deeply worried that the ideal of self help can be corrupted by manipulating the policy environment to encourage self-help initiatives for the wrong reasons. The *right* reasons include people coming together to support each other through some crisis or where there is obvious mutual inter-dependence such as child care. But what could happen is, as cutbacks occur in other direct care provision, more and more service users are imposed onto those self-help groups. This need not happen if voluntary and self-help agencies are vigilant, are tough in negotiating deals, or if appropriate levels of funding can be established. Stopping a government committed to cutbacks will always be difficult, but the voluntary sector must establish some mechanism for monitoring funding against perceived need, especially at a time of relatively high inflation. This information must then be disseminated to all voluntary agencies as a way of assisting them to strike bargains on care provision which they are content to accept.

The communitarian philosophy outlined here, containing as it does a major contribution from the voluntary ethic, is not a weak-kneed submission to whatever government suggests that communities should provide. The communitarian approach is intent on building competent communities and enhancing the ability of local groups to assist each other and their neighbourhood. Part of being competent is the ability, as a community, to negotiate and respond to proposals from central and local government. The enabling local authority – after all, elected by those communities in the first place –

must be part of an open-minded, 'cards on the table' discussion in which the community, enhanced by strategies to empower local groups, is able to strike effective local deals.

The National Council for Voluntary Organisations (NCVO) and similar organisations must provide the voluntary sector with the skills and abilities to undertake these negotiations whilst, at the same time, promoting at a local level the empowerment and networking arrangements so crucial to the voluntary sector. Voluntary agencies themselves must become more capable of defining community needs and involving service users, in order to speak authoritatively on behalf of those communities. Only by developing strategies for user involvement and empowerment will the voluntary sector be taken seriously by local government and health authorities. The voluntary sector must also promote not-for-profit activity as a way of countering the burgeoning private sector and in managing local activity for social result.

Another implication of this discussion is the need for agencies to think carefully about their advocacy and service role. Trying to remain an advocacy agency whilst developing extensive services can create tensions. In the mid-1980s, MIND dealt with this in a way which caused some confusion. Everything became advocacy. The scheme developed was useful for an agency primarily concerned with advocacy, as the national office of MIND has always been. For local mental health associations and those authorities with which they were in contact, however, the creation of a policy in which everything was seen in an advocacy framework was not always helpful. MIND's distinction suggested that advocacy might be either formal or informal. In other words, it could either speak directly on behalf of individuals professionally or through public policy statements, *or* provide advice and assistance to individuals privately thus enabling them to obtain the best possible help, care or support.

Another way of looking at it is to suggest that advocacy can be *personal* (working with and on behalf of individual service users); *professional* (speaking on behalf of service users, for example, in MIND's case representing patients at mental health review tribunals); *public* (for example, campaigning for more resources for mental health care); and *practical* or exemplary advocacy (providing innovative or catalytic services and demonstrating new needs and approaches). It was in the latter area where confusion began. Should a local association of MIND only run new and innovative services and demand that health and local authorities take over the running of these if they prove to be successful? Or should the local association continue to run such services if they are helpful to users? Sticking to an advocacy position might be seen by some as indulgent, by others as courageous. It all depends on the organisation being clear as to what it wants to do. Developments of contractual arrangements for services suggest that, in future, many voluntary organisations will not be permitted the luxury of setting up a new, exciting service in the hope that the local authority will take it on. Voluntary organisations will have to accept that they are in the business of long-term care.

Issues to Be Addressed

A number of important issues emerge from this discussion. First, the advocacy–service conflict; second, the role of volunteers in an increasingly professional and contract-based environment; and third, the way in which new services are begun and continued.

The Advocacy-Service Conflict

The first issue is not readily resolved unless an agency has clear objectives and, in some cases, splits into two components: the service-providing part and the advocacy agency. Many local authorities have begun to recognise the need to fund third-party advocacy organisations which will do nothing else but speak up on behalf of, and with, service users. Possibly citizens advice bureaux may take this on as an additional function, or councils for voluntary service may see it as an appropriate role. In many places, service-user or disability groups are the natural custodians of such advocacy and ought to be funded accordingly.

Some agencies have tried to continue an advocacy function whilst developing significant services, and have begun to come unstuck. One recent example will suffice. A local organisation for people with mental handicaps has developed out of a parent-based, local MENCAP society. During the 1970s, it developed two strands: one the effective delivery of residential care, day activities and employment services; the other, help and advocacy for people with learning disabilities. Rapid expansion of the agency in the early and mid-1980s on the basis of non-inflation-proofed grants, left the organisation running a significant deficit on some of its housing projects. In order to bring these projects back into balance, it was necessary to change the way in which the services were provided from a 'normalised' approach (using well-paid, highly motivated care workers) to a more traditional outreach service (using a team of care assistants). During these changes, the advocacy role of the organisation was more or less lost. Who was to speak for, and on behalf of, the people the organisation traditionally served? Although token representation of people with learning disabilities on the committee allowed some communication, the financial position was such that effective management action had to be taken and the progressive (and, to some extent, overly idealistic) views of care provision were set aside. To be fair to the staff, their anxiety at the financial position, their own job insecurity, and what may be perceived as bad management, were intimately bound-up with their deep concern for the quality of life of those who they were employed to support. Nevertheless, when the chips are down, it is job security and salary which take first place; only independent advocacy on behalf of the users can ensure that their views are listened to.

This short description of the difficulties of one voluntary organisation is not intended to criticise its management and staff. They have worked hard to provide a relevant service for people with mental handicaps at a time of great difficulty financially, when both the local borough and funding from central government and health authorities were being severely constrained. Problems like these might well affect more voluntary organisations in future, and lessons must be learned now rather than in five or ten years' time.

Voluntary organisations which tender for services and contract with local authorities must do so with a clear head and an open mind, negotiating deals which are fully acceptable to them, and ensuring that they are not forced down a road they do not wish to take. Incidentally, it is worth noting that the MENCAP group described above has continued to involve a very large number of volunteers, by creating a philosophy which is at once progressive and humanitarian, supportive and empowering of service users. The organisation runs residential care, leisure and recreation services, employment and day activities. The localised nature of this care, and the exciting and personally rewarding aspects of working with children and adults with learning disabilities, attract volunteers, both young and old. To continue to do so, as services become more contractual, probably requires the organisation to see itself as embodying the voluntary ethic through helping to empower the local community and making it more competent. This will be essential, in any event, if the organisation is to ensure that people with learning disabilities are integrated into the local community.

An organisation which appears to have found a solution to the advocacy–service dichotomy is the Newham parent-to-parent network. Established in 1975, the Parent Centre now runs 12 programmes covering a wide range of educational activity using volunteers. The centre has a work co-operative, integration and support services for people with disabilities, runs an education helpline and provides a range of training courses. All this has developed from extensive parent networking aimed at providing advocacy and support to parents whose children with special educational needs were being assessed. Fun days, counselling and family support are all included. In addition, the centre provides a community publishing resource and a tutor outreach service to children and adults needing help with literacy. While assisting people to speak for themselves and speaking up for them, the centre also runs a range of services. These twin functions mesh together well because they are part of, and grew out of, a local community network. The potential conflict is minimised through the full participation of all involved.

One evident danger of community care is a large number of small, isolated services – residential care in group homes of five or six, day care in segregated units, and so on. The ideal is to create a far more flexible approach which encourages people with disabilities to use the existing and ordinary facilities of the community. These will include local education authority, adult evening institutes, libraries, ordinary recreational facilities (such as swimming baths and sports centres), the local pub, and so on. A vital role of the voluntary sector is to help the community to become more accepting of people who are perceived as different. That means building communities which are generally more competent to absorb and support people with significant disadvantages.

The general tenor of the last few paragraphs is, of course, relevant to all those who have been segregated. The voluntary sector has the same role to play in enhancing integration of black and white, men and women, young and old. The black voluntary sector will, quite properly, provide a range of services for the black community, often because, by default, the white voluntary sector has claimed to be egalitarian yet has failed to provide relevant services. At the same time, the challenge for the black voluntary sector is to encourage participation in the community and thus to encourage sharing and interdependence.

An inherent danger of the contractual approach is the fragmentation of community care into a range of small agencies reflecting the variety of disability groups, minority ethnic groups, and so on. A key function of the enabling local authority will be to encourage, catalyse and support multiethnic and multiracial groups concerned with community enhancement and to enable 'black-specific' agencies to be established. For example, Ujima and Carib Housing Associations, or the Afro-Caribbean Mental Health Association have provided a focus for, and met the needs of, the black community in a way which traditional white agencies had failed to do.

The 'white' voluntary sector also faces that challenge. In the past, too much lip service and too little action have meant that voluntary agencies have undertaken the process of equal opportunities without necessarily achieving the outcomes to match. Voluntary agencies will have to develop new strategies to achieve the objectives implied here.

The Voluntary Sector in the Contract Culture

The second issue, identified earlier, is the role of volunteers in an emerging 'contract culture'. Some are worried that volunteers will have to be drafted as 'make-weights' when the contract price does not cover the costs of care. Few people volunteer to work with private agencies. If voluntary organisations begin to resemble private contractors will volunteers still come forward? And will the trade unions resent the increasing intrusion of volunteers into places traditionally the preserve of paid workers?

The Volunteer Centre has for many years been concerned about paid-work 'substitution'. In 1975 a committee chaired by Geoffrey Drain produced guidelines which have proved a useful basis for policy. Recently, the centre has begun updating these guidelines in the light of changes outlined here. The new draft includes the following:

- any change in the level of voluntary activity should be preceded by full consultation between interested parties;
- agreements on the nature and extent of volunteering should be widely known;
- voluntary work should complement, not substitute, paid work;
- actions of volunteers should not threaten the livelihood of paid staff.

This sort of formulation is clearly very helpful for both statutory and voluntary agencies. More worrying, is their relevance to the 'contract culture'. Voluntary organisations will have to think carefully about any agreements; cautiously balancing price, volume and quality. In some instances, quality may only be achieved, at a particular price, by supplementing paid staff with volunteers – a possible recipe for friction, and reducing the voluntary nature of volunteering to a 'required' component of care. This could rapidly de-motivate volunteers, with a consequent drop in standards of care. Only some clarity at the outset will enable voluntary agencies to take on contracts which they can sustain.

Establishing New Services

The third issue is that of establishing new services. Many voluntary organisations have, in the past, wanted to establish innovative schemes and then hand them over to statutory agencies. A long and honourable history exists of such transfers. During the 1980s, the likelihood of this occurring had diminished. More and more voluntary agencies that identify new needs are left to run services, often with declining grant aid from local government or health authorities.

Many examples exist of services which were established by voluntary agencies under some kind of collaborative arrangement. Future contracts may not change the nature of such services very much, but are likely to have a significant effect on small 'minority interest' services which currently struggle along on pitiful grant aid. An example of the former category is LOROS (the Leicestershire Organisation for the Relief of Suffering). NAHA and NCVO (1987) describe this as a good example of collaboration between a voluntary organisation and a district health authority. LOROS was pioneered 10 years ago by a local GP to provide hospice care. It presented its case for financial support to the local health authority who were sufficiently impressed to provide a letter of intent encouraging LOROS to undertake fundraising while detailed discussions were held. By 1983 sufficient resources had been obtained to develop services.

LOROS operates both a day centre and counselling service, and in the mid-1980s opened a 25-bed hospice. This is managed by a committee comprising 14 members, of whom 6 are nominated by LOROS, 6 by the health authority, and 2 are independent. Both capital and revenue costs are shared. The hospice site was provided by Leicestershire District Health Authority with professional support, such as architects, being provided by Trent Regional Authority. The district health authority pays 80 per cent of the hospice's revenue costs and LOROS the remaining 20 per cent. A terminal care service of this kind is not often provided by health authorities. In this case, the commissioner–supplier relationships which may develop following the NHS Review White Paper (Department of Health, 1989) will simply formalise the contractual position in relation to the funding provided by the district health authority. Whether this would be the case with my second example of collaboration, considered below, is a moot point.

Hackney advocacy scheme is an innovative project developed initially by City and Hackney Community Health Council (CHC). Its purpose is to stress the value of empowerment through patient advocacy. The CHC Women's Group, concerned about the high level of deprivation amongst the ethnic minority population in Hackney, ran a campaign to set up a health project. They were particularly concerned that parental mortality in Hackney was twice the national average. Funding was received from the health authority and inner city partnership money. It was, as the NAHA/NCVO report points out, a good example of how a CHC can act as a focus for community initiative and establish a partnership with a health authority, using external finance. The scheme has four objectives:

- to improve the physical health of non-English-speaking women and their babies;
- to develop a support system for them;
- to improve race relations in the NHS locally;
- to help hospital staff understand special needs of this group.

Unfortunately, inner city partnership money is of short-term duration. Whilst the LOROS hospice scheme described above received long-term, substantial funding from the health authority, the Hackney Ethnic Minority Project was established with relative financial insecurity and much less funds. Under the new contract culture, there are both opportunities and threats. If the project is seen to be an important component of meeting the health needs in Hackney, the health authority (as the commissioner of health care) could set up a long-term contract with the project to provide services and support to women in Hackney. In doing so, it could empower and enable that project to go beyond its initial remit and enhance the ability of the ethnic minority community to assist those in need. On the other hand, the health authority could simply ignore such a project as being peripheral to the main stream of health care and too small to warrant a contractual relationship.

The last example illustrates perhaps the most important issue for the communitarian ideal and for the development of local, not-for-profit activity. A health project, like that in Hackney, is crucial to local community empowerment and to enhancing the ability of local people to provide effective care and support. By demonstrating the ability of such a not-for-profit project to perform a valuable service, the voluntary sector can show how the 'contract culture' can empower local people and, among other things, improve the health care of the population. This requires health and local authorities to recognise the significant, inherent potential of such schemes. If they do not, not only will they miss an opportunity, but they might also kill off embryo projects which have immense local possibilities. In summary, the voluntary sector must make itself visible if it is to build on the work it has done in recent years and to demonstrate that the 'contract' culture has a future.

CHAPTER 7

A LONGER VIEW: THE FUTURE ROLE OF THE VOLUNTARY SECTOR

A New Social Order

It is a truism that the seeds of the future are buried in the past. Sometimes we do not recognise those seeds until they flower in a most unexpected way. Fifteen years ago the postwar consensus on the welfare state seemed to many to be still intact. Full employment was still a goal; the 'social wage' was an important component of everyday life. Nevertheless, the seeds of significant change had already been sown, though the changes still came as a great surprise to many people. Notions of pluralism in welfare provision were being discussed in the 1970s. It is unlikely, however, that many people thought the current Conservative government would go as far as reorganising the NHS three times in a decade, ending up with proposals for internal markets and hospitals being given the opportunity to be self-governing. Nor did the welfare state consensus imagine that a government would deliberately engineer a rise in unemployment of 200 per cent in an attempt to control union power and to boost an individual rather than collectivist philosophy.

Many activists within the housing field were shocked at the government's ruthless determination to sell off council housing and, during the early 1980s, were still organising a campaign for a new homeless persons Act in which anyone, including single persons with no dependants, would be entitled to accommodation. Although the government has not, in fact, repealed the Housing (Homeless Persons) Act 1977 (now incorporated in the Housing Act 1985), it has done so in practice. Few local authorities with significant problems of homelessness have the housing stock to provide for more than a tiny number of those who need housing.

The response of the voluntary sector has been predictably confused. Many of the more active, radical voluntary organisations have been affronted by government changes which have reduced the availability of housing, increased poverty, attacked state provision in welfare, and appeared to be on the brink of dismantling statutory services such as the NHS. Some have given a cautious welcome to the new consumerism focusing on individual need, but many have only done so in a half-hearted manner, preferring to see negative implications rather than positive opportunities. Indeed, there is no doubt that significant constraints will emerge from the current government's policies.

Opportunities do exist, but there are now more people homeless than ever before; and more people living below the poverty line than for decades. There are more people who feel generally insecure in their jobs (for example, male suicide has almost doubled since 1979); and more people feeling the lack of decent transport (particularly in the south-east), with clogged roads and the everyday stress of getting to work. There are the pressures on informal carers to take over even rudimentary services theoretically provided by central and local government. In the face of this list of difficulties, it is sometimes hard to be positive and to recognise the opportunities which *do* exist.

Looking into the Future

It is also true that the sudden changes which have occurred have caught many people off balance. Charles Handy (1989), in his recent book *The Age of Unreason*, believes that we are moving into an era of increasingly divergent thinking and 'discontinuous' change, that is, changes are taking place immediately rather than gradually, with little or no policy discussion or precedent. He believes that the world of work is changing, for example, by creating new organisations with a core and a periphery, and that over the next 20 years only half of those currently employed full-time will be in a similar employment. The rest will either be working for themselves or will have put together 'portfolios' of different jobs. Many of the demographic changes now affecting British society will also have effects which are difficult to predict.

Various reports during the last 15 years have pointed to the increasing number of elderly and very elderly people. In 1975 it was predicted that by the year 2000 there would be an increase of around a million in the number of people over 75. Much of that change has already occurred. The same source suggests that the number of over 85s will increase by around 250,000 from 1990 to 2000 (OPCS, 1983). At least 20 per cent of these elderly people will suffer from dementia, many will need help in taking a bath or with other domestic arrangements, and a large proportion will require 24-hour care. At the same time, the number of school-leavers is dramatically reducing. From a peak in the early 1980s, the number of 15- to 18-year-olds leaving school will reduce by over half a million by the mid-1990s (Central Statistical Office, 1989, table 1.1). There will, therefore, be an insufficient number of young people to go into such professions as nursing. Health authorities and local authorities have been making contingency plans for some time. The serious shortfall of student nurses, for example, could have significant consequences.

Any grey cloud has a silver lining. One person's loss may be someone else's gain. In this case, health authorities are already encouraging older women to return to the workforce, and it is likely that retirement age will be lifted, at least informally if not statutorily. As people live longer, they may be able to work longer, whilst having the option to retire if they wish. Greater equality in the workplace may ensue from women returning to work and being able to demand reasonable remuneration. The reduced numbers of young people could also affect wage levels, however. In the mid-1980s massive changes in the financial markets led to huge salaries being paid to young people in accountancy, law and financial management, massively distorting wage patterns (in the south-east, particularly). This, in turn, led to a house-price spiral (fuelled by a badly timed reduction in the availability of double mortgage interest relief), the reverberations of which are only now settling down around the country. Perhaps another increase in wage rates for young people is imminent in the early 1990s. Yet, at the same time, the advent of 'telecommuting' (working from a computer terminal at home) which is a spin-off effect of information technology, may, as Charles Handy (1989) suggests, lead to more people working from home, with all sorts of unintended consequences. One of these would be that if more people became computer literate and able to do their own typing, the number of office juniors and secretaries required would be reduced. At the same time, house prices might even-up around the country as workers would not be required to travel to work so frequently and could choose where to live.

Some of the changes will take place quickly; some much more slowly. Telecommuting, for example, is not likely to catch on as quickly as some believe because people like working together from a common base. Nonetheless, greater freedom and possible changes to patterns of the working week may allow some to work within their local communities, volunteering for a variety of tasks. Young people may be less in evidence within voluntary organisations; the middle-aged and elderly more visible. Many elderly people will be relatively well-off – the 1990s being the first time that a large cohort of elderly people will both own their own homes and have occupational pension schemes.

All these changes will mask significant pockets of deprivation – geographically and socio-economically. Those who have benefited from the last 20 years will reap the rewards of escalating house prices, inflation-linked pensions, and so on. There will, however, still be those who require help, support and attention. For example, those who have remained tenants; those with disabilities which remove the opportunity for well-remunerated employment; those who are homeless; or those who have been unable to drag themselves (because it is still the government's dominant ideology to get on your own bike, not someone else's) out of the cycle of disadvantage. Perhaps the most important questions we can try to answer are the following. First, can all the changes that have occurred, or are predicted to occur, be steered in such a way as to benefit disadvantaged people while society continues to obtain the benefits of increased personal effort and responsibility? Second, what role should the voluntary sector play?

The Future Role of the Voluntary Sector

In a world which is changing so rapidly, the greatest danger for the voluntary sector is to just wait and see, reacting to the changes and agendas set by others. Being able to react positively, swiftly and firmly is essential, though any reaction must be principled and assertive, based on a clearly articulated programme for the sector. More than ever before, voluntary organisations require a manifesto for the future – a common agenda of their own, built on a set of principles in which they believe and which offers the ability not only to respond flexibly to change, but also to engineer that change in a way which the sector feels is right. The voluntary ethic in community care is concerned with a balance of giving and receiving, with participation and empowerment, with the encouragement of citizenship through volunteering and voluntary activity, with running services for local people managed by local people, and with the underpinning of a society in which individuals matter within an interdependent whole.

Chapter 4 showed that the voluntary sector comes close to, but does not match, a communitarian ideal. In developing a manifesto, some vision of society is required. Achieving that vision then becomes the sector's objective, and describes a set of goals. If the communitarian ideal as a vision worth fighting for is accepted, then the role of the voluntary sector in steering society towards a reappraisal of its values will emerge. Nothing less is sufficient. Many will argue that the voluntary sector is only there to provide certain services, perhaps those which the statutory sector has not got round to or has not noticed are required. That is too narrow a view, however; and the world does not stand still.

A greater emphasis on individual worth and need puts a premium on consumer choice and consumer power, tempered with an acceptance that individuals are not isolated actors on a hostile stage, but part of the wider social fabric. The voluntary sector should therefore grasp that communitarian ideal and develop a manifesto which has three main strands. The first of these would be a critique of the trends which currently influence thinking and their long-term implications (chapter 6 discussed what those might be); the second, to develop a clear vision of society in the twenty-first century; and the third, to develop a flexible strategy for the voluntary sector in achieving that vision.

Criticism of Current Policies

A number of criticisms of current policy have already been described. Forward planning has not made allowances for the increasing number of elderly people, the reduced number of school-leavers in the 1990s, and the widening disparities of wealth and income. On average, society will be better off, but pockets of deep deprivation will remain. The individualism which has been so applauded is all very well for those who, at any one moment, are successful, but creates greater anxiety and feelings of insecurity in others. Egalitarian attitudes to wealth creation – and there *is* a non-racist and non-sexist component to capitalism – are insufficient if they lead implicitly to a widening economic gap between ethnic, religious, or gender groups. 'The age of unreason' may be exciting for those who can ride the changes, but provokes considerable distress in those caught out or who see the world turned upside down around them. Perhaps the most damning indictment of current trends, however, is the tendency towards an atomised and overly competitive society, the members of which do not see themselves as part of a broader community.

Any criticism of this kind may seem like a throwback to past decades. Are we not just hankering after the good times? Perhaps we find change much more difficult than we might think? Certainly, it is true that we must be open-minded and flexible, and able to accept the changes which are before us. Nevertheless, the most damning objection to recent individualism is that it sees some people as being inherently of greater human worth than others. We should rather accept a phrase coined by Tom Campbell (1988) that people are of 'equal worth but unequal worthiness'. In other words, every person is of equal human worth and importance as a human person, but may be more or less worthy of different care or support interventions, depending on his or her needs and requirements.

A New Vision

Our vision of a communitarian society rests on encouraging individual worth and freedom within an interdependent society. The political left has begun to grasp this, as is shown, for example, by the Labour Party policy review. Relinquishing nationalisation in favour of highly constrained social ownership is a trend from socialism to communitarianism; another is the move towards one member, one vote. In many ways, the British Labour Party is beginning to match the social democratic policies of European centre-left parties. Sweden, for example, has for many years had an effective partnership between, on the one hand, individual freedom, private production and capitalist effort and, on the other, a high taxation which enables the state to offer a high social wage and extensive social services. Many of these services are provided by state payment for private and not-for-profit production.

The communitarian vision suggested here is important for the voluntary sector because it is close to, though does not entirely match, the sector's traditional aims. One important difference between this vision and that usually provided by all political parties is a less authoritarian stance. Too frequently, even those politicians who say that they believe in consultation behave as if they know best. Consultation is often tokenist – a disabled person or a black person co-opted onto some committee or other. Indeed, all political parties seem unable to give up the reins of power, regardless of how much they talk of participation. However, opportunities do exist to grasp the changes which have occurred – changes which potentially can devolve power and resources to local people – and to demonstrate the way in which people can be involved locally. The vision offered here is of a plural society with a burgeoning not-for-profit sector. Some of this sector will be traditional voluntary agencies, some will be more aggressively entrepreneurial in pursuit of 'social result'.

A crucial factor will be the control of such organisations. Voluntary agencies or not-for-profit concerns must be more than 50 per cent in the hands of those who have no pecuniary interest in that organisation. At the same time, steps must be taken to ensure efficient and effective management, and to obtain the best possible outcomes for the resources deployed. There is nothing inherently capitalist in being efficient, particularly in the provision of care, especially when resources are scarce, and likely to remain so. There is nothing intrinsically socialist in demanding interdependence, together with an emphasis on not-for-profit activity (which, note, includes statutory agencies!). Private agencies will remain in the social care field. But if the community is to be truly empowered through the provision of money by the enabling state there should be less need for private care.

This vision demands that a lot of help is given to local agencies in the fields of management, personnel, organisation and administration, which ought to be funded by central or local government. Too often in the recent past, voluntary organisations have been expected to take on 'projects', sometimes quite well funded, but without any administrative help. The advent of contractual arrangements may well ameliorate this position to some extent, but, on the other side of the coin, voluntary contributions may be needed to underwrite services where the contracted payments will not meet the organisation's minimum standards of quality.

Two modes of contract are possible: contracting-in, where voluntary organisations are involved in planning and are able to influence their role in the pattern of local care; and contracting-out, in which the local or health authority tenders for work which may or may not be won by a voluntary organisation. Contracting-in leads to better-planned services; contracting-out perhaps to greater choice and efficiency. In the Netherlands, government subsidies for voluntary organisations have risen sharply during the 1980s. Here, the model being developed is known as an 'incorporated model', where agencies enter into close financial relationships with the state, becoming more or less quasi-public services.

In many ways, the communitarian ideal is concerned with a holistic concept of health. The World Health Organisation (WHO) has promoted the idea of intersectoral collaboration, which recognises the contribution which different sectors make to the well-being of society. Let us take one example. Much research evidence suggests that psychological and emotional problems in children are related to a variety of factors. Among these are living in high-rise housing accommodation; insecurity of tenure; lack of good leisure facilities, particularly open space; poverty; and a lack of pastoral care in schools. Good housing is obviously crucial to a child's development, and it could be assumed that a safe playspace is just as important. Few may realise, however, that a supportive school environment (where children are treated as equals, regardless of intellectual ability, and where a quasi-family support is provided) is also vitally important to minimising psychological problems, particularly in adolescence.

When it is pointed out, this seems obvious – of course, people cannot be compartmentalised into the bit that goes home, the bit that plays football, the bit that goes to the cinema, and the bit that goes to school. Nevertheless, that is precisely how our services are run. Education is divided off from housing which, in turn, is separated from environmental and leisure provision which, in turn, is not seen as part of the promotion of health. WHO's Healthy Cities movement and its report, *Health for All by the Year 2000* (WHO, 1975) are designed to rebuild a 'new public health'. Underpinning this movement is a belief that people are interdependent, and that the services and support which they receive should likewise interact. This, too, is part of the communitarian vision.

Similarly, the voluntary sector's role must be interactive. Indeed, the voluntary sector can cut across current administrative or bureaucratic boundaries, working within a community to bring together housing, education, or environmental concerns. One key role for the voluntary sector is to show the way in intersectoral collaboration, by doing it better than statutory authorities.

A Flexible Strategy

If the ideal is communitarian, intersectoral, collaborative and interdependent, then this sets a significant challenge for the voluntary sector. Voluntary agencies are too often aggressively independent; fight for their grants like any capitalist private organisation would fight for its market; are still too paternalistic, authoritarian and professional; do not involve consumers to anything like the extent that they should; and are insufficiently embracing of local people. There are exceptions to the latter point. Self-help groups, local church groups and localised community organisations often are able to act as flexible social networks. But as such organisations become larger or more formalised they often lose that ability. Table 2 (see pages 78–9) suggests some characteristics of the current voluntary sector and the proposed features of a vision of society in the twenty-first century which were outlined on pages 70–2. If we try and match both sets of features, we can begin to form a strategy for voluntary sector activity in the 1990s, as set out below.

Such a strategy will place an emphasis on the involvement of services users and participation. Organisations will encourage the users of their services to become the managers and owners of those services. Organisations will become far more participative, not only encouraging and empowering local people, but also acting as a channel for resources to further support that empowerment. Voluntary organisations will be concerned to create freedoms and to support individual effort and activity. There is nothing wrong with 'gaining from giving', but the encouragement of freedom should be within a framework which reduces anxiety and maximises the mental health of the population. That can only be achieved through genuine democracy, participation, and the development of a range of opportunities for people which are properly funded by an enabling state and are under the control of those who have no pecuniary interest in the development of care. Voluntary agencies will probably want to see certain legislation of the last decade repealed – for example, that which enacted the recommendation by the Widdicombe Report (1986) to restrict local councillors from being involved in agencies funded by local government. At the same time, careful audit, monitoring and regulation will be needed to ensure that those who might seek to obtain personal gain are unable to do so.

Voluntary agencies must be cautious about taking on difficult tasks in order to prove their social virility. This danger was pointed out by Diana Leat *et al.* (1986) in a Policy Studies Institute report. Voluntary organisations, they said,

in their desire for recognition (and funds) sometimes seem all to willing to conspire with the statutory sector in the view that the voluntary sector can do the impossible but miracles take a little longer. Voluntary organisations should have the confidence to

Table 2 *Key strategic requirements for the voluntary sector in moving from its current to future role*

Voluntary Organisations Now	Strategy for Change	Communitarian Vision – Future Role of the Voluntary Sector
Voluntarily established	• demand/offer support to establish new not- for-profit organisations • involve community in new developments	catalysed, assisted, negotiated
anarchic	• develop community responsibilities • liaise with local authorities in contracts	not-for-profit activity on behalf of the community
responsive but limited – single issue, old-fashioned	• extend range/research need • more flexible personnel policies	responsive but flexible
sometimes planned	• research community need • work with statutory agencies on health/care requirements	planning on basis of need

Table 2 *continued*

Voluntary Organisations Now	Strategy for Change	Communitarian Vision – Future Role of the Voluntary Sector
fragmented, plural	• encourage effective regulation/ monitoring	regulated, plural, comprehensive
advocacy	• involve service users in planning and management • spilt advocacy/service in some places	assisted options, improved self and citizen advocacy, clarity of community objectives
paternalistic	• user involvement • bottom-up, person-centred planning	participative
too professional	• ensure professionals recognise their role as helpers	professional-user dialogue and agreements
concerned with special interest group or cause	• wider community responsibility through regulation and participation	collective/ individual, interdependent

suggest that although, under the right conditions and with the right resources, they may be able to do the impossible miracles are not on offer. (p.136)

Even though voluntary agencies can achieve 'the impossible', this can only be done with extensive support. Health authorities and local authorities will have to see the necessity for providing local umbrella groups, such as councils for voluntary service (CVS), with grant aid in order to develop industrial relations expertise as a support service to local voluntary endeavour. CVS could also provide marketing help, public relations and press facilities, personnel management expertise, and financial and management support. Or voluntary agencies may obtain these from the private sector if they know where to look. Perhaps local CVS should act as brokers, pointing voluntary organisations at relevant professional organisations or firms, such as solicitors, accountants, and so on.

Training will be another vital area during the next few years. Many voluntary organisations have small training budgets and are unable to buy in the type of training required by their staff. Training requirements in the voluntary sector are no different to those in the private sector. Front-line staff need appropriate training in their caring task; management require training in management skills and techniques, as well as overall help with the strategic management role. A key issue during the next decade will be the extent to which voluntary organisations can develop their ability to negotiate contracts in order to get the best deal possible for themselves and their clients. All of this will have to be done in the context of a wider strategic approach to shift the voluntary sector from its current approach to that which better meets the communitarian position.

Table 2 sets out some of the key points in such a strategy. Chapter 4 described how the voluntary sector might be steered into a better path by hijacking the trends from the old statism and attaching them to the new communitarianism. If it is to do so, the voluntary sector must change. The centre column of table 2 sets out key changes for voluntary organisations. From being voluntarily established organisations, the voluntary sector will have to accept the need for new organisations to be established to meet specific needs. Statutory agencies will have to use a judicious mixture of grant and contract to help set up new organisations to create the range and choice required by the consumers. The voluntary sector must accept these developments whilst, at the same time, demanding effective regulation and monitoring to create a managed market. Although some of the worst fears of those who dislike the market mentality can be discarded, there is no doubt that complete freedom of competition for social care will not work.

Voluntary organisations will also have to develop a wider sharing and a greater community responsibility. Some are already good at this, but others do not collaborate and share as much as they should. It will be necessary, too, to involve the community much more, and for voluntary organisations everywhere to make far greater efforts to talk to local people. Community health councils, for example, although statutory agencies, are largely run by volunteers. These volunteers make far too little effort at present to get out into the community, to determine community reactions, and to involve the community in the future direction of the health service.

The voluntary sector will also have to get involved in researching need, and working alongside those statutory agencies which are the purchasers of care. The NHS Review proposes that district health authorities become 'insurers' or 'commissioners' of health care, determining the needs of the community and buying in care from a range of agencies (including self-governing hospital trusts) appropriate to their perception of need. Voluntary organisations (whether they are to be contracted-in, or provide services which are contracted-out) must get to know those needs, too, so as to be able to negotiate hard and effectively with statutory agencies.

Above all, it will be necessary to move from the old paternalism and the quasi-professionalism of too many voluntary organisations to something far more participative and concerned to support advocacy by disabled and disadvantaged people. Voluntary organisations must make every effort to learn from each other how to involve disabled people at all levels within their organisations. It is not always easy to take people with significant disabilities into a management role. People with learning disabilities may have problems in understanding the way committees work; deaf people will need appropriate aids to be able to deal with meetings; blind people will require minutes on tape or in braille. People with mental health problems may fluctuate in their ability to concentrate and involve themselves in management issues. Because a person may become very disordered for a period of time does not mean that all people with mental illnesses are similar, or even that that individual cannot later resume his or her rightful role in influencing the organisation. Local people generally should also be taken far more into the confidence of statutory and voluntary organisations. However, this will be really effective only when resources and budgets are

devolved as far as possible to local communities, who must be
encouraged to set up not-for-profit enterprises to run the services
they require.

This strategy requires a major change in how voluntary organisations perceive themselves, and the way local and central government perceives the community. Some of the trends are already here,
as we have seen; others need to be encouraged. None of it will be easy,
but the voluntary sector has a greater role to play now than ever
before, both as advocate and service provider. Voluntary agencies
will need extensive support from NCVO and other umbrella groups,
which must accept this new world and begin planning to provide the
management, personnel, finance and contractual expertise that
voluntary organisations require. NCVO is already working on these
problems, but is unable to put as many staff onto the work as is
demanded by the changes. Already we can see one operation working
on a shoe-string trying to assist other shoe-string organisations. That
is a recipe for disaster.

The Challenges Ahead

If central and local government are serious in their intention to create
choice and consumerism in health and social care, then they have also
to be serious about the support they give to voluntary organisations
in trying to meet those aspirations. By and large, people do not want
for-profit organisations providing the bulk of social care. Indeed, the
private sector cannot get into the community in the way that is needed
and described in this book. Only by supporting not-for-profit activity
on the basis of the communitarian approach outlined above can
government get the best of both worlds – an enhanced and more
competent community, providing care efficiently without dumping
disadvantaged people onto unsupported relatives. There is an
opportunity to use the money currently locked up in large institutions
and statutory organisations, and to use it much more productively
through local effort. That is the challenge for local government.

Although this book has been about the voluntary ethic in
community care, it is also about the attitude of central and local
government to the Pandora's Box of consumerist welfare they have
opened. The Conservative government must recognise that it cannot
go right down the line of an individualist, anxiety-ridden state of
competitive individuals where the poor and disabled are left to starve
on city streets. On the other hand, Labour and other opposition

parties cannot simply reassert the old statist notions about public funding of public production. Whichever of the two main parties forms the government of the early 1990s, it will have to create both a greater consensus in health and social care, and a fuller consensus morality. The voluntary sector is probably the only vehicle by which that local dialogue can take place.

The voluntary sector is on the brink of massive change. There will be some who cannot cope and will hark back to the old authoritarian days of small grants and sherry with the chair of social services. There will be those who cannot get into gear quickly enough and will watch the private sector take over health and social care. And there will be those who are prepared to grab the trends as they occur, and steer them into a new direction. The scope for voluntary sector and not-for-profit activity in the 1990s is immense. It will *not* be expansion just for its own sake, but principled entrepreneurial activity aimed to make the most of opportunities on behalf of the community. Being *of* the community can assist in empowering the community to provide better services and support for disadvantaged and disabled people. At the same time, the voluntary sector can assist in devising a new shared morality – a highest common factor of our collective conscience. Nothing less will do.

Select Bibliography

Audit Commission (1986), *Making a Reality of Community Care.*

Berthoud, R. (ed.) (1985), *Challenges to Social Policy*, Gower and Policy Studies Institute.

Bosanquet, N. (1983), *After the New Right*, Heinemann.

Brenton, M. (1985), *The Voluntary Sector in British Social Services*, Longman.

Campbell, T.D. (1988), *Justice*, Macmillan.

Campion, P., Pearson, M., Stanley, I., and Tulloch, E. (1988), 'Self help in primary care: preliminary findings of a study in Liverpool', *Journal of Royal College of General Practitioners* (October).

Central Statistical Office (1989), *Social Trends*, HMSO.

Connelly, N. (1988), *Care in the Multi-racial Community*, Policy Studies Institute.

Department of Health (1989), *Working for Patients*, Cm 555, HMSO.

Departments of Health and Social Security (1989), *Caring for People: Community Care in the Next Decade and Beyond*, Cm 849, HMSO.

Gladstone, F. (1979), *Voluntary Action in a Changing World*, Bedford Square Press.

Griffiths, Sir Roy (1988), *Community Care: An Agenda for Action*, HMSO.

Handy, C. (1989), *The Age of Unreason*, Business Books (Century Hutchinson).

Hayek, F.A. (1960), *The Constitution of Liberty*, University of Chicago Press, Chicago.

Hillery, G.A. (1955), 'Definitions of community: areas of agreement', *Rural Sociology*, vol. 50, pp. 20–35.

Kinnock, N. (1986), *The Future of Socialism*, Fabian Society pamphlet no. 509.

Kymlicka, W. (1989), *Liberalism, Community and Culture*, Clarendon Press.

Leat, D., Tester, S., and Unell, J. (1986), *A Price Worth Paying?* Policy Studies Institute.

McNaught, A. (1987), *Health Action and Ethnic Minorities*, Bedford Square Press.

Mellor, H. (1985), *The Role of Voluntary Organisations in Social Welfare*, Croom Helm.

National Association of Health Authorities and National Council for Voluntary Organisations (NAHA/NCVO) (1987), *Partnerships for Health*.

Office of Population Censuses and Surveys (OPCS) (1983), *1971 and 1981 Census, Population Projections, Government Actuary mid 1983, Based on OPCS, PP2, no. 13 1983, 2023*, HMSO.

Titmuss, R. (1970), *The Gift Relationship*, Penguin.

Titmuss, R. (1976), *Commitment to Welfare*, Allen & Unwin.

Tönnies, F. (1963), *Community and Society*, ed. and trans. by C. Loomis, Harper Torchbooks, New York.

Walzer, M. (1983), *Spheres of Justice: A Defence of Pluralism and Equality*, Blackwell.

Webb, A. (1985), 'Alternative futures for social policy and state welfare', in Berthoud, R. (ed.), *Challenges to Social Policy*, Glover and Policy Studies Institute.

Widdicombe Report (1986), *The Conduct of Local Authority Business: Report of the Committee of Inquiry into the Conduct of Local Authority Business*, Cmnd 9797, HMSO.

Willmott, P. (1986), *Social Networks, Informal Care and Public Policy*, Policy Studies Institute.

Wolfenden Committee Report (1978), *The Future of Voluntary Organisations*, Croom Helm.

World Health Organisation (1975), *Health for All by the Year 2000*, WHO, Geneva.

Index

Other titles in the **Society Today** series:

Peter Newell
Children Are People Too: The Case Against Physical Punishment

Walter Schwarz
The New Dissenters: The Nonconformist Conscience in the Age of Thatcher

Colin Ward
The Child in the City

Colin Ward
Welcome, Thinner City: Urban Survival in the 1990s

John Withington
Shutdown: The Anatomy of a Shipyard Closure

For further details, please write to the sales manager, Bedford Square Press, 26 Bedford Square, London WC1B 3HU.